D. Caroline Coile, Ph.D.

Whippets

Everything about Purchase,
Care, Nutrition, Behavior,
Training, and Exercising

With 51 Full Color Photographs

Illustrations by Michelle Earle-Bridges

D1051588

BARRON'S

About the Author

Caroline Coile is an award-winning author who has written articles about dogs for both scientific and lay publications. She holds a Ph.D. in the field of neuroscience and behavior, with special interests in canine sensory systems, genetics, and behavior. A sighthound owner since 1963, her own dogs have been nationally ranked in conformation, obedience, and field-trial competition.

Photo Credits

Barbara Augello: front cover; Laura Baker-Stanto: page 93; Jane Bishop: page 81; Paulette Braun: pages 20 top, 24 top, 32, 64 bottom; Kent and Donna Dannen: inside back cover, pages 5, 16 top, 21 bottom, 44, 45, 57, 68 top, 80, 88; Dale Jackson: inside front cover, pages 9 bottom, 24 bottom, 69, 89; Iva Kimmelman: back cover, pages 33, 56 bottom, 64 top, 73; Jean Krikorian: page 41; Michael Ross: pages 20 bottom, 48 top, 56 top; Judith Strom: page 29; Studio on Wheels: page 9 top; Toni Tucker: page 13 top; Paola Visintini: pages 8, 16 bottom, 21 top, 25, 36 top and bottom, 49, 52 top and bottom, 53 top and bottom, 61, 65 top, 68 bottom.

All inquiries should be addressed to:
Barron's Educational Series, Inc.
250 Wireless Boulevard
Hauppauge, NY 11788
http://www.barronseduc.com

ISBN-13: 978-0-7641-0312-4
ISBN-10: 0-7641-0312-1

Library of Congress Catalog Card No. 97-46536

Library of Congress Cataloging-in-Publication Data
Coile, D. Caroline.
    Whippets : everything about purchase, adoption, care, nutrition, behavior, and training / D. Caroline Coile ; illustrations by Michele Earle-Bridges.
        p.   cm.—(A complete pet owner's manual)
    Includes bibliographical references (p.   ) and index.
    ISBN 0-7641-0312-1
    1. Whippet. I. Title. II. Series.
    SF429.W5C65   1998
    636.753′2—dc21   97-46536
                                                          CIP

Printed in China

19 18 17 16 15 14 13 12 11

Important Note

This pet owner's guide tells the reader how to buy and care for a Whippet. The author and the publisher consider it important to point out that the advice given in the book is meant primarily for normally developed puppies from a good breeder—that is, dogs of excellent physical health and good temperament.

Anyone who adopts a fully grown dog should be aware that the animal has already formed its basic impressions of human beings. The new owner should watch the animal carefully, including its behavior toward humans, and should meet the previous owner. If the dog comes from a shelter, it may be possible to get some information on the dog's background and peculiarities there. There are dogs that for whatever reason behave in an unnatural manner or may even bite. Only people that have experience with dogs should take in such animals.

Caution is further advised in the association of children with dogs, in meeting with other dogs, and in exercising the dog without a leash.

Even well-behaved and carefully supervised dogs sometimes do damage to someone else's property or cause accidents. It is therefore in the owner's interest to be adequately insured against such eventualities, and we strongly urge all dog owners to purchase a liability policy that covers their dog.

Contents

Preface

Honey joined our family when she was about a year old. She was a Whippet, our first sighthound, and we were her third owners. I was six years old then and have shared my life with sighthounds ever since.

Sometimes I wonder why. She taught me—the hard way—to keep my favorite stuffed animals up high. She taught me how to clean dog doo-doo off the carpets. She taught me to never tie a dog's leash to my bicycle handlebars and try to ride really fast. She taught me the pleasure of walking on the beach—alone, because she invariably deserted me to run home once she felt we had gone far enough.

However, she also taught me how fun it was to be a partner in adventure with a Whippet. I learned how to explain what a Whippet was to the countless passersby who stopped to ask, "Is that a baby Greyhound?" I told my friends she was a deer; a few even believed me. Most of all, I learned to appreciate the Whippet as one of the earth's most shapely, sweet, and swift creations.

One day, Honey followed a car to the road, where a neighbor saw a station wagon pull over and call Honey into it. We never saw her again, and we never stopped looking for her. This book, in a sense, is the culmination of that search.

I've written books about many other breeds of dogs in the interim, but this one about Whippets is a favorite. It's a favorite because few other breeds of dogs exist that I can recommend so whole-heartedly as a family compan-ion. Still, Whippets are different, and they have very different needs from the run-of-the-mill dog. After all, we were Honey's third owners because the first two couldn't cope with her, and they couldn't cope with her simp because they were never told how. The goal of this book is to tell how: how to find a good Whippet, how to train, feed, and care for it, how to cope with problems, how to have fun and how to make a fast friend for life

Acknowledgments

The information contained in this book comes from a variety of sources breeders, original research, scientific articles, veterinary journals, and a library of dog books. But by far my most heartfelt gratitude must go to my most demanding teachers, who have taught me the skills of both home repair and dog repair, allowed ample testing opportunities for behavioral problem cures, and whetted my curios ity (and carpets) about everything canine for the past 20 years: Baha, Khyber, Tundra, Kara, Hypatia, Savannah, Sissy, Dixie, Bobby, Kitty, Jeepers, Bean-Boy, Junior, Khyzi, Wolfman, Stinky, Honey, and Luna.

A book is more than written words; it is the product of the efforts of many dedicated and talented people— illustrator, photographers, copy-editor, technical evaluator, typesetter, and many more of whom I remain blissfully ignorant. The person responsible for orchestrating this chaos is the editor. While every contributor has played a vital role in the creation of this book, it is to Mary Falcon, my editor at Barron's, that I am indebted for making my contribution seem like the easy par

The Poor Man's Racehorse

Snuggled amid a sea of pillows, a Whippet dreams. Eyelids flicker and paws twitch in a wild chase across an endless dreamscape. A look of sublime contentment blankets the soft face, because this is Whippet utopia, a combination of the best things in Whippet life: hedonistic luxury and running amok. The Whippet honestly comes by the desire to run with reckless abandon, descending from generations of dogs bred for speed. Its legendary quest for creature comforts seems to have been added on its own prerogative, however. For all its courtly manners and elegant lines, the Whippet is a member of the nouveau riche, emerging from the humblest of origins.

The double-suspension gallop has two phases when all four feet are off the ground.

Greyhound Downsizing

The Whippet may have inherited its regal aspirations from its remote ancestors, the coursing dogs of ancient Egypt. Dogs of undeniable Greyhound form are depicted on the tombs of ancient pharaohs who lived over 4,000 years ago. This ancient family of Greyhound-like dogs are known as sighthounds, because they rely on sight to spot and run down game. They are the fastest of dogs. Different sighthound breeds have been developed through the ages to cope with different climates, terrain, and quarry. Sighthounds have long appeared in a range of sizes from the diminutive Italian Greyhound to the lofty Greyhounds, Deerhounds, and Wolfhounds.

Sighthounds have in common a body build that combines relatively long legs, a narrow torso, and a flexible, slightly arched spine. This conformation enables them to use a bounding, or double-suspension, gallop when they run, similar to what a cheetah uses. Most other dogs run like a horse: at full speed there is one period (when the feet are all contracted under the body) when all four feet are suspended off the ground. In the double-suspension gallop, a second suspended phase occurs when the feet are fully extended in front of and behind the body. This style of running allows for explosive speed but not a lot of endurance.

Fleet sighthounds have always found favor with nobility for their sporting pursuits. While the pharaohs were coursing their full-sized Greyhounds, a smaller version was decorating their living quarters. Some claim—though no direct evidence exists—that these small Greyhounds were the ancestors of today's Whippets.

The Greyhound flourished in medieval Europe, continuing its reign as the nobility's sporting hound, but little record of the smaller Greyhounds persists. In England, royal forests became hunting preserves for the aristocracy. In the eleventh century, the Forest Laws may have been indirectly responsible for the increased popularity of smaller Greyhounds among commoners. Though a great variety of game was hunted within the royal forests, the stag was the ultimate prize. The Greyhounds favored for hunting stag were large and robust. Smaller Greyhounds would not have been favored and would probably have been culled or returned to the commoners who had raised them.

The Forest Laws imposed dire penalties for commoners or their dogs caught hunting in the royal forest. To prevent the commoners' cast-off Greyhounds from hunting, those kept within 10 miles (16 km) of the royal forest had to be lamed, either by chopping off several toes or severing a ligament in the knee. Non-Greyhounds or small dogs were not required to be lamed. Perhaps the cast-off Greyhounds were crossed with each other or with other breeds so that their progeny would have a less obvious Greyhound look, and thus not be victims of laming.

While the Greyhound was the choice for hunting sport, the little Greyhound mixes earned their keep by hunting for the pot. They proved themselves adept as ratters and poacher's companions, and as rabbit and hare catchers extraordinaire. Not until 1832, when the Reform Act finally allowed nonlandholders to hunt more than just vermin with dogs, could the

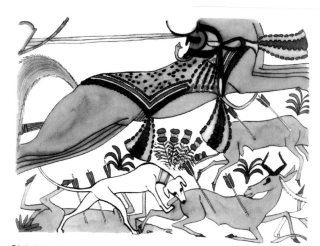

Sighthounds are among the most ancient families of dogs.

little Greyhounds flaunt their virtues. By then they had found their niche.

These still were not Whippets. In fact, the rare references to Whippets seemed to refer to Greyhound-Spaniel crosses, not to any true breed of miniature Greyhounds. The nineteenth century finally saw small Greyhounds come into their own as sporting dogs in their own right.

The Quick and the Dead

The sport of rural commoners has historically been centered around betting on contests between animals, including bear and bull baiting, ratting, and dog fighting. The common workers could not ride to the hunt, so they initially unleashed their fastest dogs to chase captured rabbits. Eventually *snap dog* competitions became popular, in which bets were made on which dog could *snap up* the most rabbits within a large circle drawn on the ground. The British excelled at breeding vermin-catching dogs. The same know-how was put to use in developing fast, agile, and uncannily quick

The double-suspension gallop in action.

dog with a tenacious desire to chase any small, moving animal. Exactly which dog breeds went into the mixture is unknown. Undoubtedly, Grey-

Dubbed the poor man's racehorse, *the Whippet provided entertainment and companionship for the colliers of northern Britain.*

hounds or descendants of Greyhound castoffs from the days of the Forest Laws were the major contributors. Most breeders believe some ratting pit dogs and terriers were added for their quickness and gameness (and in turn, the Whippet's influence can be seen in some modern terriers). The result was a small dog with a Greyhound build that was the quickest dog the world had ever seen.

Fleet and Sweet

With the advent of the industrial revolution, the masses of rural workers who moved to urban industrial centers brought with them the animal sports they enjoyed. Sports involving dogs were the most amenable to city life. Those who had enjoyed betting on enclosed coursing soon found that rabbits weren't necessary; the dogs would chase just about anything, including a waving rag. Betting on *rag dog* races became a consuming passion among the coal miners of northern Britain.

A good running rag dog was a great source of pride in a family that could boast of little other wealth. Such dogs would be coddled and treated as well as—or better than—any other family member. Their value made them targets of theft, and a good running Whippet that wandered was likely to be stolen. In the region's chilly climate, the dogs also earned their keep as bedwarmers. Thus, the Whippet's temperament was formed not only through selection for running ability but also for the inclination to stay close to its family and maybe even to burrow under the covers—the world's first heat-seeking missiles.

Were the coal miners' rag dogs the descendants of some ancient miniature Greyhounds? Were they the descendants of the Greyhound castoffs from the Royal Forests? Or were they created de noveau as the snap dog and rag dog of the 1800s? Those questions will probably never be answered. Today's Whippets, however, can confidently trace their origins to these *poor man's racehorses* of the Welsh coal miners.

From Rags to Riches

During the late 1800s, exhibiting dogs became popular among the upper classes in England. New breeds were eagerly sought, registered, and exhibited. Whippets joined their ranks as an officially recognized breed in 1891, and for the first time in its history, appearance was important. Judicious crosses with Italian Greyhounds may have helped the Whippet achieve its stated ideal: a Greyhound in miniature.

Whippet interest was also growing in America; in fact, the American Kennel Club registered its first Whippet three years earlier than the Kennel Club in England. By the early 1900s, both Whippet showing and racing were being enjoyed by the upper crust of the Western world, and the Whippet had wheedled its way into high society. It wasn't until after the First World

Today's Whippet is more likely to be a pampered pet living in the lap of luxury with its doting caretakers.

Whippets are often mistaken for Greyhounds, but are much smaller, as evidenced by the difference in size between this large male Whippet and small female Greyhound.

9

The Long and the Short of It

Because the early snap and rag dogs were bred for performance rather than appearance, they came in a variety of coat types. By the time Whippets were eligible for conformation exhibition, however, they were predominately smooth coated, although a few wire-coated Whippets remained. The latter were not very popular. They were eventually lost from the breed, in part because the original breed standards called for a dog that looked like "a Greyhound in miniature"—and Greyhounds were smooth coated.

In the 1980s, an attempt was made to introduce long-coated Whippets into the breed. Controversy ensued, with the long-coated Whippet advocates claiming the long hair dogs resulted from inbreeding of dogs carrying recessive, long-coated genes and opponents claiming they were the result of crossbreeding. The American Whippet Club ultimately disallowed the long-coated Whippets. A beautiful breed in its own right, these dogs were then renamed *Silken Windsprites* and are now gracing the rings of rare breed shows.

War, however, that Whippets began to become popular with people from all walks of life.

The Whippet has since become a steady favorite as a cherished pet, consummate racer, and graceful show dog throughout the world. Like a diamond formed from coal, it is a priceless gem formed of humble ingredients, shaped by great pressures, and brought to the world by hardworking miners. And like a diamond, it sparkles and enriches the lives of all it touches.

The Whippet Whim

Sighthounds are notoriously not for everyone. They are exasperatingly independent, often aloof, and have a tendency to run away.

Whippets are sighthounds. Their racy outline and zest for speed define the very essence of the sighthound family. However, they are unlike most sighthounds in one important aspect: they obey! Whippets are well suited as pets for *almost* anybody.

They are not suited for people who want a rough-and-tumble dog, a dog for protection, a swimming companion, or an exclusively outdoor dog. They are not for people who spend all their time in polar climates. Nor are they for people who don't believe in leashes. They are, after all, sighthounds deep down.

For the majority of people, though, Whippets are ideal pets.

The Whip-Pet

Temperament: Whippets are wise, whimsical, winsome, and wonderful. They like nothing better than to rest securely snuggled beside or on their owner's lap. They have a penchant for following their owners from room to room, resting their heads upon their special person's arm or leg, and staring soulfully into that person's eyes whenever activity slows enough to allow it. Some people find the Whippet too "clingy" for their lifestyle, but most people enjoy the Whippet's desire to be close.

Whippets are every bit as gentle in action as they are in appearance. They are patient with children and kind with one another. However, this gentleness renders them vulnerable to mishandling by unsupervised children and injury by unfriendly dogs.

If raised with cats or even rabbits, or introduced to them slowly, they can become close friends, though they may forget this friendship if they see the cat or rabbit streaking across the yard.

Whippets are playful, but not as relentlessly playful as many other breeds. If you want a dog to keep your children occupied for hours, find another breed. Whippets may chase a ball a few times, but probably won't bring it back after the first time. Of course, they seldom tire of a game of "catch me if you can." That's because they never lose. Some Whippets have found fame as frisbee fanatics, but don't expect your Whippet to naturally show an interest in catching discs without training.

For some people, the Greyhound is too big, the Italian Greyhound is too small, but the Whippet is just right.

Among the gentlest of breeds, Whippets make loving and obedient companions, forming deep attachments with their family.

The favorite Whippet game is chasing something. The sight of a moving lure can turn the laziest hound dog into a shrieking, quivering, crazed beast. That's great if you want to participate in lure-coursing or racing. It's not great if you want to let your Whippet mosey around the front yard with you while you garden. A cat, squirrel, or even a blowing scrap of paper can arouse the chasing instinct, and your Whippet will not be able to control itself. It will chase whatever small object it sees moving over the ground. Your Whippet will chase that object wherever it goes—all too often into the path of a moving car.

It's not that Whippets are disobedient. It's just that they can't be trusted. They can't be trusted because they are too fast and can find themselves in the middle of the road before they even seem to realize how they got there.

On all counts, Whippets are extremely obedient. Their quiet, calm nature makes them a natural at obedience lessons. They can *sit, come, heel, stay,* and *lie down* (just not on a cold, hard floor) with the best of them. They don't take harsh corrections well, but they don't need them either. Whippets are among the most successful of all hound breeds in competitive obedience. The caveat is that hound breeds are, in general, not very competitive at obedience trials!

Whippets are not noisy dogs and will seldom bark without reason. Some won't even bark with reason, making them less-than-ideal watchdogs. Most, however, will voice the alarm announcing an uninvited dog or other intruder in the yard. Their propensity to greet all strangers with a wagging tail or at worst, a look of annoyance for awakening them, makes them worthless as guard or protection dogs.

The Whippet's most dangerous weapon is its tail. Anyone who has been hit by it wagging at vision-blurring speed will have their own theory about the origin of the Whippet's name—a tail whipping can raise welts on human legs and clear coffee tables.

Exercise: The Whippet is an athlete, not a decorative figurine. If you can't treat it to daily exercise, then you are better off with one of the many lovely Whippet statues available.

Can a Whippet live in an apartment? Surprisingly, yes. The Whippet spends most of its day storing up the vast energy required for its explosive bursts of speed. In other words, it sleeps a lot. However, you must give it a chance to burn off that energy every single day. This means either a very ong walk or the chance to career at breakneck speed in a safe, fenced area. It will enjoy jogging to an extent, but remember that the Whippet is a sprinter, not a marathon runner.

Upkeep: The Whippet coat is wash-and-wear. No fancy haircuts or extensive brushing is ever required; in fact, you would be hard pressed to think of anything to groom on a Whippet. For the grooming obsessed, this may be a downside, but for most people, this is a blessing. Whippets have very short, close-fitting hair that naturally repels dirt. A damp rag or some no-rinse shampoo will do the trick in most cases. Best of all, Whippets have virtually no doggy odor!

Housing: You won't need a dog-house or a kennel run for your Whippet simply because it plans to be spending its leisure hours curled in your coziest chair. You may, in fact, have to buy a chair just for your Whippet—or at least some heavenly soft bed. The Whippet is on a constant quest for softness and warmth. If your home is soft and warm enough for you, add a few pillows and more than a few degrees, and it will be satisfactory for your Whippet.

Although a Whippet should never be expected to live outside, they do occasionally have to venture outdoors to perform their bodily functions (even Whippets have them, though they would have you believe otherwise) and to stretch out and run. Since their entire body is built on the coiled spring design, not surprisingly they are among the world's best fence jumpers. As long as they are outdoors, Whippets are on the lookout for something to chase, and that something is usually not in your yard. Thus, unless you plan to walk your Whippet on a leash every time it goes out, plan to get a fence, and plan to make it tall.

Aesthetics: The Whippet silhouette is far from subtle. People either love

Although it may look like a work of art, the Whippet is more than a statue to decorate your home—it is a living being that requires exercise and attention every day.

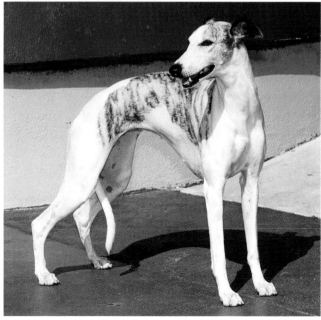

A breed of graceful curves, elegant lines, and powerful build.

the graceful curves and svelte physique or they find it bizarre. People in the latter group simply have bad taste, so their opinion shouldn't matter to those in the former group, who obviously have good taste. People in both groups will find the Whippet's soft doe eyes irresistible.

Health: Whippets are unusually healthy in the world of purebred dogs. No serious hereditary problems plague the breed. This is not to say that Whippets are disease-free or that no hereditary problems exist—just that such problems are few and far between. The hip, joint, eye, heart, and bloating problems so prevalent in many breeds are virtually unheard of in Whippets.

The most common hereditary problem is cryptorchidism, which is the failure of one or both of the testicles to descend into the scrotum. This is hardly a life-threatening conditioning for the average pet, but such dogs are not allowed to compete in conformation shows. In addition, undescended testicles have an increased risk of developing testicular cancer, so they should be surgically removed.

Some dilute gray-colored (called *blue*) Whippets have thin or partially absent hair, a condition often accompanying dilute coloration in many breeds. Some pink-skinned, white-haired dogs seem more susceptible to demodectic mange, but most have perfectly healthy skin.

Many people worry that the Whippet is delicate. In some senses that is true. It has thin skin and is prone to lacerations. It has little body fat and easily becomes chilled. It propels its body at enormous speed, and once in a while, it crashes. Usually, it rolls a few times and keeps on running. Sometimes it breaks something. The most common running injury is an abraded foot pad, however.

With good care and good luck, Whippets typically live 12 to 14 years, with 16 years not being unusual. So take your time choosing your partner for the next decade.

Which Whippet?

Before embarking on your search for a Whippet, take a moment to clarify exactly what traits are most important for your new dog. Most people insist upon good looks, good temperament, and good health. Some people also want promising coursing, show, or obedience potential.

Good looks: You want your Whippet to look like a Whippet, which means it will need to have at very least some of the more important Whippet characteristics. The Whippet is a medium-sized dog with a slender, athletic build, resembling a Greyhound in miniature. Its coat is short and sleek, its legs long and slender, its body supple and curvaceous. Its ears fold back when relaxed and are semipricked

The Whippet resembles the Greyhound in miniature. Points of a typical Whippet are (1) large eyes, (2) folded ears, (3) sleek coat, (4) small waist, (5) arched loin, (6) athletic build, and (7) deep chest.

hen attentive. Its eyes are large and lustrous. These traits are the minimal requirements; more exacting requirements are set forth in the Whippet standard of perfection (see Appendix).

Good looks and conformity to the official standards also require sound body structure. Soundness refers to the ability to move in an efficient manner so that your Whippet can run hard and long without laming itself. Unsound Whippets may have feet that point outward rather than forward, may have legs that interfere with each other when trotting, or may have any number of structural faults that result in an inefficient stride. Although complete soundness is a trait more vital to the show or coursing dog than to the pet, it should nonetheless not be ignored.

The appearance of the sire and dam of the litter is the best indication of the looks of their offspring. Good breeders will have photos of the entire family available. By examining the pedigree for conformation champions, you can also get an idea of how well your dog's ancestors conform to the official standards.

Temperament: Whippets have earned their position as one of the most popular sighthounds because of their stable temperament. Most Whippets do have excellent temperaments, but you should still take some precautions when choosing your future partner.

Again, the personality of the sire and dam are the best indicators of their offspring's personality. The Whippet is naturally reserved with strangers, but it should not act afraid or aggressive. A dam with very young puppies may act protectively; if so, she should be revisited when the pups are a little older.

The presence of obedience titles in the pedigree indicate not only obedient ancestors but breeders who care about temperament. Equally important is the environment in which the puppy is raised. Pups raised with minimal (or aversive) human contact during their critical period of development (from about six to ten weeks of age) may have some lifetime personality problems.

Good health: Your prospective puppy should:
• Have its first vaccinations and deworming.
• Be outgoing and active. Avoid a puppy that shows signs of fearfulness or aggressiveness. If a pup is apathetic or sleepy, it may have just eaten, but it could also be showing signs of sickness.
• Be clean, with no missing hair, crusted or reddened skin, or signs of parasites. Eyes, ears, and nose should be free of discharge.
• Have pink gums; pale gums may indicate anemia.
• Have no indication of redness or irritation around the anus.
• Not be coughing, sneezing, or vomiting.
• Not be thin or potbellied.
• Not be dehydrated, which can suggest repeated vomiting or diarrhea. Test for dehydration by picking up a fold of skin and releasing it. The skin should pop back into place.
• Have two testicles in the scrotum (if male)

Quick Picks

Finally, the fun part: deciding what color, sex, and age Whippet is best suited for you. These choices are all just part of personal preferences; you really can't go wrong.

Color choices: The sampling of Whippet colors should provide something for everybody. Whippets can be solid colored or parti-color (spotted). The color pattern on either can be clear or brindled (color broken up by irregular, vertical, black stripes). The color hue can basically be black or red. Finally, the color saturation can be intense or dilute. The dilute colors are less favored by some show exhibitors.

"May I go home with you?" This pup is the picture of health.

Thus, a Whippet might be a parti-color blue brindle; that is, a white dog with patches of dilute black (light gray) with darker gray stripes. It could also be a solid fawn, which would be a dog that was a dilute red with no brindling or white spotting. Visit a large Whippet gathering and enjoy all the combina-

A red brindle parti-color (front) and a dilute fawn brindle parti-color (rear).

tions before choosing a favorite. However, one warning: you may decide you have to have one of each, and that's a lot of Whippets!

Male or female? The differences between male and female Whippets are slight compared with those in most breeds. Whippet males are slightly larger, 19–22 inches (48–56 cm) at the shoulder. Females are about 18–21 inches (46–53 cm) tall. A large male could weigh as much as 35 pounds (16 kg), while a small female could weigh as little as 20 pounds (9 kg).

Both males and females tend to get along well with one another. Males may be slightly sweeter, but some may think nothing of repeatedly lifting their leg on your furniture to mark your house as their territory. On the other hand, females come in estrus (*season* or *heat*) twice a year. This lasts for three weeks, during which time you must keep your female away from amorous neighborhood males who consider your house a singles bar. You must also contend with her bloody discharge and possible attempts to elope with her suitors. The solution for both sexes is neutering (see page 76).

Puppy or adult? The easiest transition time for puppies is between eight and 12 weeks of age. However, if you definitely want a competition-quality dog, you may have to wait for a puppy five or six months of age. An adult Whippet may need a longer adjustment period. No matter what the age, if the puppy has been properly socialized (that is, treated gently and exposed to a variety of situations, people, and dogs), your Whippet will soon blend into your family life and love you as though it's always owned you.

Puppies are not for everyone, however. No one can deny that a puppy is cute and fun, but a puppy is much like a baby; you can't ever be too busy to walk, feed, supervise, or clean (and clean and clean). Whippet puppies are hellions and can gnaw their way through your home with astounding speed, apparently aided by ricocheting off the walls. If you work away from home, or have limited patience or heirloom rugs, an older puppy or adult may be a better choice.

Breeders may have older retired show or competition dogs available that would relish the chance to live as a pampered pet. The American Whippet Club has a rescue group devoted to finding homes for Whippets in need of a loving home.

Quality: Dogs are generally graded as pet, show, and breeding quality. The Whippet has additional grades: coursing and racing quality. A pet-quality dog is one that has some cosmetic flaw that would prevent it from winning in the conformation ring but still has good health and temperament. Most such flaws would never be noticeable to the untrained eye. The most common reason in Whippets is the failure of both testicles to descend in males. Being a pet is the most important role a dog can fulfill, and pet quality should never be belittled. Show-quality dogs should first of all be pet quality; that is, they should have good temperament and health. In addition, they should portray the attributes called for in the breed standard, so they could be expected to become champions in the show ring. Breeding-quality dogs come from impeccable backgrounds and are of even higher quality than are show- or working-quality dogs. Breeding quality means more than the ability to impregnate or conceive. Far too often, though, these are the only criteria applied to prospective parents by owners unduly impressed by a registration certificate. It is difficult to pick a show-quality puppy at an early age; it is impossible to pick a breeding-quality puppy.

Puppy checkpoints: pink gums, clear eyes, clean nose, clean ears, clean anus, tight skin, no protruding ribs, no potbelly.

The better quality you demand, the longer your search will take. A couple of months is a reasonable time to spend looking for a pet puppy, a couple of years for a breeding-quality dog. Begin your search for a high-quality Whippet by seeing as many Whippets as possible, by talking to Whippet breeders, by attending Whippet competitions, and by reading every available Whippet publication.

A final note of caution: registered puppies should come with a pedigree and either a litter registration certificate, individual registration certificate, or statement in writing clearly stating why such documents are not being supplied. Some unscrupulous breeders promise to provide these documents "soon" and never deliver them. The registration materials should already be available by the time the puppy is ready to leave for its new home.

Social Graces

Today's Whippets are likely to be found gracing the finest homes, a long way from the stark surroundings of their forebears. The Whippet has always expected to be a real member of the family, sharing family activities, and of course, the family home. In turn, Whippet owners expect their charges to act civilized, not using the antique furniture as a chewbone or the heirloom rugs as a bathroom.

Your Whippet now faces the transition from canine litter member to human family member. Every day will be full of novel experiences and new rules. Your pup is naturally inquisitive and will need you to guide it toward becoming a well-mannered member of the household.

The Whippet Welcome Waggin'

Half the excitement of welcoming a new dog is preparing for the big homecoming. Much of the fun comes from a Whippet accessory buying spree. The best sources for supplies are large pet stores, dog shows, and discount pet catalogs. Your welcome basket should include:

• Buckle collar: for wearing around the house. Avoid leather, which can stain the coat. A wide, soft collar is more comfortable for the dog than a narrow, stiff collar.

• Wide nylon choke or martingale collar: safer for walking on lead. Whippets can back out of buckle collars.

• Leash: nylon, web, or leather—never chain! An adjustable show lead is good for puppies.

• Lightweight, retractable leash: better for older adults; be sure not to drop the leash as it can retract toward the pup and could frighten it.

• Stainless steel food and water bowls: avoid plastic; it can cause allergic reactions and hold germs.

• Cage: large enough for an adult to stand up in without having to lower its head. See page 20 for a description.

• Exercise pen: tall enough that an adult can't jump over or, preferably, with a top. See page 21 for a description.

• Toys: latex squeakies, fleece-type toys, ball, stuffed animals, stuffed socks, empty plastic milk or soda jugs. Make sure no parts of toys, including squeakers or plastic eyes, can be pulled off and swallowed.

• Chewbones: the equivalent of a teething ring for babies.

• Antichew preparations, such as Bitter Apple: the unpleasant taste dissuades pups from chewing on items sprayed with it.

Buckle, choke, and martingale collars.

- Baby gate(s): better than a shut door for placing parts of your home off-limits. Do not use the accordion style gates—a dog can get its head stuck and asphyxiate.
- Soft brush.
- Nail clippers: guillotine-type is easier to use.
- Pooper scooper: two piece rake-type is best for grass.
- Dog shampoo (see page 74 for choices).
- First aid kit (see page 86 for contents).
- Food: start with the same food the pup is currently eating.
- Dog bed: a round cushion is heavenly, but you can also use the bottom of a plastic cage, or simply use an entire cage—both well-padded.
- Sweater or coat for cold weather.

Whipping Up Mischief

Your puppy will naturally want to explore every nook and cranny of your house. Part of the pup's exploratory tools are its teeth. Any chewed items left in its wake are your fault not your pup's—you are the one who should have known better. Harsh corrections are no more effective than a tap on the nose along with a firm *No* and removal of the item. If you come across one of your cherished items chewed to bits and feel compelled to lash out, go ahead—hit yourself in the head a few times for slipping up. It may teach you a lesson!

Any place your Whippet may wander must be Whippet proofed. The first step is to do everything you would do to baby proof your home. Get down at puppy level, and see what dangers beckon.
- Puppies love to chew electrical cords in half and even lick outlets. These can result in death from shock, severe burns, and loss of jaw and tongue tissue. Puppies can also pull electrical appliances down on themselves by pulling on cords.
- Jumping up on an unstable object (such as a bookcase) could cause it to come crashing down, perhaps crushing the puppy.
- Do not allow the puppy near the edges of high decks, balconies, or staircases. Use baby gates, temporary plastic fencing, or chicken wire in dangerous areas.
- Doors can be a hidden danger area. Everyone in your family must be made to understand the danger of slamming a door. Use doorstops to ensure that the wind does not suddenly blow doors shut or that the puppy does not go behind the door to play. Whippet tails are extremely susceptible to injuries from doors. Be especially cautious with swinging doors; a puppy may try to push one open, become caught, try to back out, and strangle. Clear glass doors may not be seen, and the puppy could be injured running into them. Never close a garage door with a Whippet running about. Finally, doors leading to unfenced outdoor areas should be kept securely shut. A screen door is a vital safety feature; Whippets are adept at bolting after a squirrel across the street when you open the front door.

Dangers also abound within the yard. Check for poisonous plants, bushes with sharp, broken branches at Whippet eye level, and trees with dead branches or heavy fruits in danger of falling. Whippets can charge around the yard at break neck speed, so you must remove anything that a leg or foot could hit. If you have a pool, be aware that although dogs are natural swimmers, you should familiarize your dog with how to get out of the pool.

Watch out for these potential killers:
- drugs
- chocolate (especially baker's chocolate)
- rodent, snail, and insect baits
- antifreeze
- household cleaners

As appealing a picture as it may make in your dreams, a Whippet as a Christmas gift (or as any unexpected gift) is a very bad idea.

- paint thinner
- toilet fresheners
- nuts, bolts, pennies
- pins, needles, and anything in a sewing basket
- chicken bones or any bones that could be swallowed
- sponges

A warm coat is a necessity in cold weather.

Before bringing your puppy home, you should decide what parts of your home will be off-limits. Make sure that every family member understands the rules, that sneaking the puppy onto off-limit furniture, for example, is not doing the puppy any favor at all. Whippets naturally consider your chairs and sofas to be their personal thrones, but if you don't want them on the furniture, keep them off from the beginning. Don't pick the pup up to sit on your lap; instead, sit on the floor with it. Never fling the pup off of furniture or use mousetraps on furniture surfaces, because both practices are dangerous and absolutely a bad idea unless you like emergency visits to the vet. Several more humane items (available through pet catalogs) emit a loud tone when a dog jumps on furniture, but these should not be necessary if you train your young puppy gently and consistently from the beginning.

Whippets don't have the body padding to enable them to be comfortable on a cold, hard, floor, so don't expect your Whippet to sleep off of the furniture unless you provide it with its own warm, soft spot. Some people give their Whippets their very own chair, others train them to get on the sofa only if their special blanket is on it, and others provide a snug bed inside a cage.

The cage (or *crate*): Many new dog owners are initially appalled at the idea of putting their pet in a cage as though it were some wild beast. At times, though, your Whippet pup can seem a wild beast, and a cage is one way to save your home from ruination and yourself from insanity. A cage can also provide a quiet haven for your youngster. Just as you hopefully find peace and security as you sink into your own bed at night, your pup needs a place that it can call its own, a place it can seek out whenever the need for rest and solitude arises.

Used properly, your Whippet will come to think of its cage not as a way to keep itself in but as a way to keep others out!

Don't expect your Whippet to stay in a cage all day, every day, while you are at work. Overuse of the cage is not only unfair, and even cruel, to the dog, but it can also lead to behavioral problems. A cage should be the canine equivalent of a toddler's crib. It is a place for nap time, a place where you can leave your pup without worry of it hurting itself or your home. It is not a place for punishment, nor is it a storage box for your dog when you're through playing with it.

Place the cage in a corner of a quiet room but not too far from the rest of the family. Place the pup in the cage when it begins to fall asleep, and it will become accustomed to using the cage as its bed. Be sure to place a soft blanket in the bottom. By taking the pup directly from the cage to the outdoors upon awakening, the cage will be one of the handiest housebreaking aids at your disposal.

The X-pen: An exercise pen (or *X-pen*) fulfills many of the same functions as a cage. X-pens are transportable, wire, folding playpens for dogs, typically about 4 feet by 4 feet (1.2 m by 1.2 m). X-pens are the perfect solution when you must be gone for a long time, because the pup can relieve itself on paper in one corner, sleep on a soft bed in the other, and frolic with its toys all over! It's like having a little yard inside. The X-pen provides a safe time-out area when you just need some quiet time for yourself. However, before leaving your pup in an X-pen, make sure that it cannot jump or climb out. Covers are available for incorrigible escapees. If you use an X-pen, cover the floor beneath it with thick plastic (an old shower curtain works well), and then add towels or washable rugs for traction and absorbency.

A breathtaking view, but a dangerous sight for a nimble sighthound, which could easily jump the railing or slip between its bars.

Whippets love the soft life: soft beds and soft toys.

21

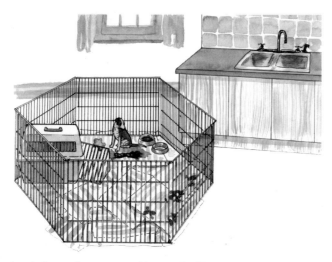

A safe haven for puppy and home: the X-pen.

some training before your pup extends the notion of den to your home.

You can use your dog's cage as its den. However, if the cage is too large, the puppy may simply step away from the area it sleeps in and relieve itself at the other end of the cage. An overly large cage can be divided with a secure barrier until the puppy is larger or housebroken. Even so, just like the wolf cubs, your puppy may step just outside the door of the cage and eliminate there, because to the pup, that fulfills the natural requirement of not going in the den. The puppy has failed to realize that it has just soiled *your* den. The more the pup soils in a particular spot, the more likely it will return to that same spot.

Housebreaking blunder #2: The second big mistake puppy owners make is to allow accidents to happen. Puppies have very weak control over their bowels. If you don't take them to their elimination area often, they may not be able to avoid soiling. Puppies, like babies, have to eliminate a lot. You can't just stick them in a cage all day while you are at work and think you won't return home to a messy cage and a messy pup. A rule of thumb is that a puppy can, at most, hold its bowels for as many hours as the pup is months old. This means that a three month old can hold itself for three hours. If the pup is forced to stay in a cage longer, it won't be able to control itself and will soil the cage; you are setting the stage for a big problem. Once puppies get used to eliminating in their cage, they may continue.

Puppies tend to relieve themselves in areas that smell like urine. This is why it is so critical never to let the pup have an accident indoors. If it does, clean and deodorize the spot thoroughly, and block the pup's access to that area. Use a pet deodorizer cleaner, and never use one containing ammonia. Ammonia is a component of

Not in the House!

Whippets aren't always the easiest breed to housebreak. However, part of the blame must go to their owners, who are often guilty of serious housebreaking blunders. Most people have unrealistic expectations of their dog's ability to become housebroken, based in part upon friends' boasting about their little genius that was housebroken at two weeks of age or something similarly ludicrous. No matter how wonderful and smart your Whippet is, it probably will not have full control over its elimination until it is around six months of age and probably won't be reliably housebroken until a year old—or more!

Housebreaking blunder #1: The number one housebreaking mistake made by most puppy owners is to give their puppies too much unsupervised freedom in the house. All canines have a natural desire to avoid soiling their denning area. The denning area is considerably smaller than your entire house, however, and it will take urine, so using an ammonia cleaner is like posting a sign that says, "Go here!"

If you cannot be with your puppy for an extended period, you may wish to leave it outside (only in warm weather and with cover) so that it will not be forced to have an indoor accident. If this is not possible, you may have to paper-train your puppy. Place newspapers on the far side of the room (or X-pen), away from the puppy's bed or water bowl; near a door to the outside is best. Place the puppy on the papers as soon as it starts to relieve itself.

A better option is to use sod squares instead of newspapers. Place the sod on a plastic sheet, and when soiled, take it outside and hose it off. By using sod, you are training the pup to relieve itself on the same surface it should eventually use outside. Place the soiled squares outside in the area you want your dog to use.

Because dogs are creatures of habit, housebreaking is more a matter of prevention than correction. To avoid accidents, learn to predict when your puppy will have to relieve itself. Immediately after awakening and soon after heavy drinking or playing, your puppy will urinate. You will probably have to carry a younger puppy outside to get it to the toilet area on time. Right after eating or if nervous, your puppy will have to defecate. Circling, whining, sniffing, and generally acting worried usually signal that defecation is imminent. Even if the puppy starts to relieve itself, quickly but calmly scoop the pup up and carry it outside (the surprise of being picked up will usually cause the puppy to stop in midstream, so to speak). You can also clap your hands or make a loud noise to startle the pup so that it stops. You can add a firm "No," but yelling and swatting are actually detrimental. When the puppy does relieve itself in its outside toilet, remember to heap on the praise and let your Whippet pup know how

Separation anxiety is characterized by lapses in housebreaking, nervous behavior, and destruction around doors and windows, particularly chewed and scratched walls, door jams, and rugs.

pleased you are. Adding a food treat really gets the point across. Keep some in a jar near the door, and always accompany your pup outside so that you can reward it.

Housebreaking blunder #3: The number three housebreaking mistake made by dog owners is overuse of punishment. Even if you catch your dog in the act, overly enthusiastic correction tends only to teach the dog not to relieve itself in your presence, even when outside. This is why you should reward with a tidbit when the pup does relieve itself outside. Punishment doesn't make clear what is desired behavior, but reward makes it clear very quickly. Punishing a dog for a mess it made earlier is totally fruitless; this only succeeds in convincing the dog that every once in a while, for no apparent reason, you are apt to go insane and attack it—a perfect recipe for ruining a trusting relationship. That guilty look you may think your dog is

"Who, me? Get into trouble?" You bet!

exhibiting is really fear that you have once again lost your mind.

Housebreaking blunder #4: The number four housebreaking mistake owners make is to open the door and push the pup outside by itself. After five minutes, the pup is let back in and promptly relieves itself on the rug. Bad dog? No, bad owner. Chances are the pup spent its time outside trying to get back inside to its owner. Puppies do not like to be alone, and knowing you are on the other side of the door makes the outdoors unappealing. In bad weather, the pup probably huddled against the door so it wouldn't miss when the door was again opened. The solution? You must go outside with the pup every time. Don't take it for a walk, don't play with it, simply go with it to its relief area, say "Hurry up" (the most popular choice of command words), and be ready to praise and perhaps give a treat when the pup does its deed. Then you can go to its play area or back inside.

As soon as you are hopeful your precocious puppy is housebroken, your pup will take a giant step backward and convince you that no link exists between its brain and bowels. If your previously housebroken adult Whippet soils the house, a physical or emotional problem could be the case. A physical examination is warranted any time a formerly housebroken dog begins to soil the house. You and your veterinarian will need to consider the following possibilities:

• Older dogs may simply not have the bladder control that they had as youngsters; a doggy door is the best solution.

• Older spayed females may *dribble*; ask your veterinarian about drug therapies.

• Several small urine spots (especially if bloody or dark) may indicate a bladder infection, which can cause a dog to urinate frequently.

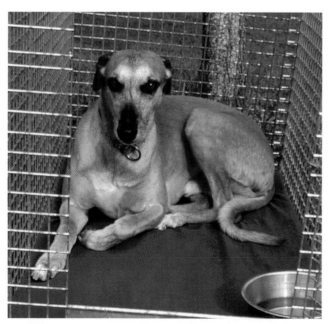

The cage can be an important housebreaking tool, and should remain as the dog's own private place. Soft bedding is a must. The wire cage can be covered for privacy and added warmth.

One of the best solutions for behavior problems is the addition of a friend.

- Sometimes a housebroken dog will be forced to soil the house because of a bout of diarrhea and afterward will continue to soil in the same area. If this happens, restrict the dog from that area, deodorize the area with an enzymatic cleaner, and revert to basic housebreaking lessons.
- Male dogs may *lift their leg* inside of the house to mark it as theirs. Castration will often solve this problem if performed before the habit has become established. Otherwise, diligent deodorizing and the use of some dog-deterring odorants (available at pet stores) may help.
- Submissive dogs, especially young females, may urinate upon greeting you; punishment only makes this *submissive urination* worse. For these dogs, be careful not to bend over or otherwise dominate the dog and to keep greetings calm. Submissive urination is usually outgrown as the dog gains more confidence.
- Many Whippets defecate or urinate due to the stress of separation anxiety; you must treat the anxiety to cure the symptom. Dogs that mess their cage when left in it are usually suffering from separation anxiety or anxiety about being closed in a cage. Other telltale signs of anxiety-produced elimination are drooling, scratching, and escape-oriented behavior. You need to treat separation anxiety (see Home destruction, this page) and start cage training over, placing the pup in it for a short period of time and working up gradually to longer times. Some dogs that suffer from cage anxiety but not separation anxiety do better if left loose in a dog-proofed room.

Don't Whip It!

Even the best dogs with the best owners can sometimes do the worst things. Too often, distraught owners get their training advice from the next-door neighbor or even dog trainers who don't have a scientific background in dog behavior analysis. Great strides have been made in recent years in canine behavioral therapy. Before despairing, consult a certified canine behaviorist, who may employ a combination of conditioning and drug therapy to achieve cure. Veterinarians can sometimes offer advice, but few are extensively trained in behavior. As a first step in any serious behavior problem, a thorough veterinary exam should be performed.

Sometimes the owner inadvertently makes the behavior worse, often through the overuse of punishment. If punishment doesn't work the first time, why do owners think that it will work the second, third, or fourth time? As the misbehavior continues in the face of punishment, the owners lay the blame on the dog.

Home destruction: One of the most common, and commonly misunderstood, Whippet behavior problems is home redecoration. Owners too often assume that the dog is angry at being left alone and seeks to spite the owner by venting its rage on the home and its contents. Owners who continue to believe this erroneous idea never cure their dogs. Remember: dogs *never* destroy out of spite.

The Whippet is an extremely devoted dog, and its owners tend to be equally devoted. They chose a Whippet in part because of the breed's desire to be close to its family. The problem for many Whippets arises when its people leave it all alone. Being left alone is an extremely stressful situation for highly social animals. They react by becoming agitated and trying to escape from confinement. Perhaps they reason that if they can just get out of the house, they will be reunited with their people. The telltale signature of a dog suffering from separation anxiety is that most of its destructive behavior is ocused around doors and windows. Most owners believe the dog is spiting them for leaving, and punish the dog. Unfortunately, punishment is ineffective because this actually increases the anxiety level of the dog, the dog both looks forward to and dreads its owner's return.

The proper therapy is treating the dog's fear of being left alone. Leave the dog alone for very short periods of time and gradually work to longer periods, taking care never to allow the dog to become anxious during any session. When you *must* leave the dog for long periods during the conditioning program, leave it in a different part of the house than the one in which the conditioning sessions take place. This way, you won't undo all of your work if the dog becomes over-stressed by your long absence.

When you return home, refrain from a joyous reunion scene. No matter what the condition of the home, greet the dog calmly or even ignore it for a few minutes, to emphasize the point that being left was really no big deal. Then have the dog perform a simple trick or obedience exercise so that you have an excuse to praise it. This takes a lot of patience and often a whole lot of self-control, but letting this situation continue is not fair to you or your dog.

Not all home destruction arises from separation anxiety. Puppies are naturally demolition dogs. The best cure (besides adulthood) is supervision. Adult dogs still may destroy items through frustration or boredom. The best way to deal with these dogs is to provide both physical exertion (such as chasing a ball) and mental exertion (such as practicing a few simple obedience commands) an hour or so before leaving your dog.

Fearfulness: One of the appeals of the Whippet is that it tends to be more of a demure, gentle soul than a brash, fearless brute. Even the bravest of

Allow a shy Whippet to approach a stranger from the rear.

dogs can develop phobias and other fears, and Whippets can have their share. The cardinal rule of working with a fearful dog is to never push it into situations that might overwhelm it.

Although usually happy to meet new friends, the Whippet is naturally a bit cautious about strangers. A few can be downright shy. Never force a dog that is afraid of people to be petted by somebody it doesn't know. This doesn't help the dog overcome its fear and is a good way for the stranger to get bitten. Strangers should be asked to ignore shy dogs, even when approached by the dog. Dogs seem to fear the attention of a stranger more than they fear the strangers themselves. When the dog gets braver, have the stranger offer it a tidbit while not even looking at the dog at first. A program of gradual desensitization, with the dog exposed to the frightening person or thing and then rewarded for calm behavior, is time consuming but the best way to alleviate any fear.

Fear of thunder is a common problem in older dogs. Try to avoid this by acting cheerful when a thunderstorm strikes, and play with your dog or give it a tidbit. Once a dog develops a thunder phobia, try to find a recording of a thunderstorm. Play it at a very low level and reward your dog for calm behavior. Gradually increase the intensity and duration of the recording.

Never coddle your Whippet when it acts afraid, because this reinforces the behavior. Your Whippet knowing a few simple commands is always useful. Performing these exercises correctly gives you a reason to praise the dog and also increases the dog's sense of security because it knows what is expected. Whether your Whippet fears strangers, dogs, car rides, thunder, or being left alone, the concept is the same: never hurry and never push the dog to the point that it is afraid.

Aggression: In some breeds, aggression often results from a dog's attempts to dominate its owners. This is virtually never the case in Whippets. Aggression is almost unheard of in Whippets, but when it does occur, aggression is more likely to result from fear. A scared dog with no route of escape will often bark, growl, or bite out of perceived self-defense.

Many dogs are afraid of children, either because they don't understand what children are or because they have had bad experiences with children. Introduce dogs and children carefully, encouraging the child to be gentle and to offer the dog a treat. Unlike in humans, where direct eye contact is seen as a sign of sincerity, staring at a dog directly in the eye is interpreted by the dog as a threat. It can cause a fearful dog to bite. Teach children not to stare at a strange dog.

Jumping up: Puppies naturally greet their mother and other adult dogs by licking them around the corners of their mouth. This behavior translates to humans, but in order to reach your face, they need to jump up on you. Sometimes owners love this display of affection but not when they are all dressed up or when company comes over. Since you can't expect your Whippet to know the difference, teach it *sit* and *stay* so that you can kneel down to its level for greetings. When your Whippet does jump up, simply say "*No*" and step backward, so that its paws meet only air. Teaching your dog a special command that lets it know that jumping up is OK (when you're in your old clothes) can actually help your dog discriminate the difference.

Shutting your dog in the other room when guests arrive will only make it more crazed to greet people and ultimately worsen the problem. The more

Teach your Whippet to stay on the ground for greetings by kneeling down to its level.

people your dog gets a chance to greet politely, the less excited it will be about meeting new people and the less inclined it will be to jump up. Have your guests kneel and greet your sitting Whippet.

Barking: Having a doggy doorbell can be handy, but a dog that will warn you of a suspicious stranger is different from one that will warn you of a cloud in the sky. The surest way to make your neighbors dislike your dog is to let it bark unchecked. Allow your Whippet to bark momentarily at strangers. Then call your Whippet to you, and praise it for quiet behavior, distracting it with an obedience exercise if need be.

Isolated dogs will often bark through frustration or as a means of getting attention and alleviating loneliness. Even if the attention gained includes punishment, the dog will continue to bark in order to obtain the temporary presence of the owner. The simplest solution is to move the dog's quarters to a less-isolated location. For example, if barking occurs when your pup is put to bed, move its bed into your bedroom. If this is not possible, the pup's quiet behavior must be rewarded by your presence, working up to gradually longer and longer periods of it being alone. The distraction of a special chew toy, given only at bedtime, may help alleviate barking. The pup that must spend the day home alone is a greater challenge. Again, the simplest solution is to change the situation, perhaps by adding another animal—a good excuse to get two Whippets!

Remember these general training guidelines:

- **Never whip it:** Striking, shaking, choking, and hanging are extremely dangerous, counterproductive, and cruel; they have no place in the training of a beloved family member. Plus, they don't work.

Exercise (both mental and physical) is a cure for many behavior problems.

- **Correct and be done with it:** Owners sometimes try to make this *a correction the dog will remember* by ignoring or chastising the dog for the rest of the day. The dog may indeed remember that its owner was upset, but it will not remember why. The dog can relate only its present behavior to your actions.
- **You get what you ask for:** Dogs repeat actions that bring them rewards whether you intend for them to or not. Letting your Whippet out of its cage to make it quit whining might work momentarily. However, in the long run, you will end up with a dog that whines incessantly every time you put it into a cage. Make sure you reward only those behaviors you want to see more often.
- **Mean what you say:** Sometimes a puppy can be awfully cute when it misbehaves, sometimes your hands are full, and sometimes you just aren't sure what you want from your dog. However, lapses in consistency are ultimately unfair to the dog. If you feed your dog from the table because it begs *just this one time*, you have

taught it that while begging may not always result in a handout; you never know, begging just might pay off tonight. This intermittent payoff also produces behavior that is most resistant to change. You could hardly have done a better job of training your Whippet to beg if you tried.

• **Say what you mean:** Your Whippet takes its commands literally. If you have taught that *Down* means to lie down, then what must the dog think when you yell *"Down"* to tell it to get off the sofa where it was already lying down or you yell *"Sit down"* when you mean sit? If *Stay* means not to move until given a release word and you say *"Stay here"* as you leave the house for work, do you really want your dog to sit by the door all day until you get home?

• **Think like a dog:** Dogs live in the present; if you punish them they can only assume it is for their behavior at the time of punishment. If you discover a mess, drag your dog to it from its nap in the other room, and scold, the dog will think either that it is being scolded for napping or that its owner is mentally unstable. In many ways, dogs are like young children; they act to gratify themselves, and they often do so without thinking ahead about the consequences. However, unlike young children, dogs cannot understand human language (except for those words you teach them). You cannot explain to them that their actions five minutes earlier were bad. Remember, timing is everything in a correction. If you discover your dog in the process of having an accident, snatch the dog up, and deposit it outside, and then yell *"No,"* your dog can only conclude that you have yelled *"No"* to it for eliminating outside. The correct order would be to say *"No,"* quickly take the dog outside, and then reward it once it eliminates outside. In this way, you will have corrected the dog's undesired behavior and helped the dog understand desired behavior.

Smart as a Whippet

Your Whippet will need some guidance in order to be a civilized member of society. You have an advantage, however. Whippets, especially young Whippets, are natural followers, not leaders. Your Whippet will elect you as its leader and will expect you to guide. With the right methods, you will find that guiding your Whippet is both fun and easy.

Dog-training methods have changed little through the years—but they should have. Old-fashioned dog-training methods based on force are difficult, ineffective, and no fun for either dog or trainer. Punishment may tell a dog what not to do, but it can't tell a dog what it should do.

Remember that your role should be that of teacher, not drill master; your goal is to teach through guidance, not punishment.

Teacher's Whippet

Whippets are very amenable to training, as long as you use only the gentlest of techniques. Do both you and your dog a favor: Don't listen to your next-door neighbor's training advice or use the same techniques your grandparents (or even your parents) used. Use the methods the professionals use, and you will be astounded by what your Whippet can learn.

Whippet Tips

• **Guide, don't force:** Whippets already want to please you; your job is simply to show them the way. Forcing them can distract or intimidate them, actually slowing down learning.

• **Train before meals:** Your Whippet will work better if its stomach is not full and will be more responsive to food rewards. Never try to train a sleepy, tired, or hot dog.

• **Happy endings:** Begin and end each training session with something the dog can do well. Keep sessions short and fun—no longer than 10–15 minutes. Dogs have short attention spans. You will notice that after about 15 minutes, their performance will begin to suffer unless a lot of play is involved. Continuing to train a tired or bored dog will result in the training of bad habits, resentment in the dog, and frustration for the trainer. Especially when training a young puppy or when you have only one or two different

Command timing diagram: first comes the name and command, then the action, then the praise, then the reward.

Well-mannered Whippets are a pleasure to live with and a credit to the breed.

when talk is directed toward it by saying its name.

Many trainers make the mistake of simultaneously saying the command word at *the same time* they place the dog into position. *This is incorrect.* The command comes immediately before the desired action or position. The crux of training is anticipation: the dog comes to anticipate that after hearing a command, it will be induced to perform some action. It will eventually perform this action without further assistance from you. On the other hand, when the command and action come at the same time, not only does the dog tend to pay more attention to your action of placing it in position and less attention to the command word, but the command word loses its predictive value for the dog. Remember: name, command, action, praise, reward!

Food For Thought

Many years ago, the idea was perpetuated that dogs should never be trained with food. Yet professional animal trainers and animal-learning scientists all knew that food training produced excellent results. Only recently has food-motivated training become accepted in training the family dog. Owners are finding that dogs learn faster, mind more reliably, work more eagerly, and have a more trusting dog-owner relationship when food motivation has been used.

Dog owners have been told for years that the dog should work for praise only, but praise alone is not really a terribly strong motivator for most dogs. Praise can become a stronger motivator by always praising immediately before a food reward is given. In this way, praise becomes a secondary reinforcer, much as a gold star on a child's schoolwork gains reinforcing value because it has been paired with other positive reinforce-

exercises to practice, quit while you are ahead! Keep your Whippet wanting more, and you will have a happy, willing, obedient partner.

• **Once is enough:** Repeating a command over and over, or shouting it louder and louder, never helped anyone, dog or human, understand what is expected of them. Your Whippet is not hard of hearing.

• **The best laid plans:** Finally, nothing will ever go just as perfectly as it seems to in all of the training instructions. Although setbacks may occur, you can train your dog as long as you are consistent, firm, gentle, realistic, and most of all, patient.

Timing is everything: The first ingredient in any command is your dog's name. You probably spend a good deal of your day talking, with very few words intended as commands for your dog. Warn your dog ment. Eventually, the dog can be weaned from the food and will come to work in large part for praise. However, food should still be given as a reward intermittently.

Food is used initially to guide the dog into position and then to reward the dog when it is in place. After the dog knows what is expected, the food is held out of sight and given to the dog only after it has performed correctly. Ultimately, the dog is weaned from getting a food reward each time but still gets one every once in a while. Such a randomized schedule (as in slot machine payoffs) has been shown to be very effective with both animals and humans.

Training equipment: Equipment for training should include a six-foot (2 m) and a 20-foot (6 m) light-weight lead. For puppies, using one of the light-weight, adjustable size show leads is convenient. Most Whippets can be trained with a buckle collar, but a nylon choke collar is also an acceptable choice as long as you know how to use it correctly.

A choke collar is not for choking! In fact, it is more correctly termed a slip collar. The proper way to administer a correction with a choke collar is with a *very* gentle snap then an immediate release. The choke collar is placed on the dog so that the ring with the lead attached comes up around the left side of the dog's neck and through the other ring. If put on backward, it will not release after being tightened since you will be on the right side of your dog for most training. The choke collar should *never* be left on your Whippet after training sessions. Too many tragic cases have occurred where a choke collar really did earn its name after being snagged on a fence, bush, or even a playmate's tooth. Allowing a dog to run around wearing a choke collar is like allowing a child to run around wearing a hangman's noose.

The correct placement of the choke collar is with the long end (to which the lead is attached) coming over the top of the dog's head from the dog's left to right side.

Because of their long legs, it may take a Whippet a little more time to fold them into a sitting position than it would a short-legged dog, but it can be done.

Quick Studies

It's never too early or too late to start educating your Whippet. With a very young Whippet, train for even shorter time periods. By the time your Whippet pup (here named "Beanie") reaches six months of age, it should be familiar with the following commands:

Watch me: A common problem when training any dog is that the dog's attention is elsewhere. You can teach your dog to pay attention to you by teaching it the *watch me* command. Say "Beanie, *Watch me*," and when he looks in your direction, give him a treat or other reward. Gradually require the dog to look at you for longer and longer periods before rewarding it. Teach *watch me* before going on to the other commands.

Tip: Teach stationary exercises on a raised surface. This allows you to have eye contact with your dog and gives you a better vantage from which to help your dog learn.

Sit: Most sighthounds, including Whippets, are not natural sitters. This doesn't mean that they can't *sit*, or

Use food to guide your Whippet's head backward and slightly up. If you position its rear end next to a wall, it will have to sit in order to reach the treat.

that they can't be taught *sit;* it simply means that they seldom choose sitting as their preferred position. After all, in the Whippet's mind, it is far preferable either to lie down and snooze or to stand up and run! Still, teaching *sit* is simple. The easiest way is to stand in front of your pup and hold a tidbit above its eye level. Say "Beanie, *Sit,*" and then move the tidbit toward your pup until it is slightly behind and above his eyes. You may have to keep a hand on his rump to prevent him from jumping up. When the puppy begins to look up and bend his hind legs, praise and then offer the tidbit. Repeat this, requiring the dog to bend his legs more and more until he must be sitting before receiving praise.

Tip: If your dog backs up instead of sits down, place his rear against a wall while training.

Stay: A dangerous habit many dogs have is to bolt through open doors, whether from the house or car. Teach your dog to sit and stay until given the release signal before walking through the front door or exiting your car.

Have your dog sit, then say *"Stay"* in a soothing voice (for commands in which the dog is not supposed to move, don't precede the command with the dog's name). If your Whippet attempts to get up or lie down, gently but instantly place it back into position. Work up to a few seconds, give a release word (*OK!*), praise, and give a tidbit. Next, step out (starting with your right foot) and turn to stand directly in front of your dog while it stays. Work up to longer times, but don't ask a young puppy to stay longer than 30 seconds. The object is not to push your dog to the limit but to let it succeed. To do this, you must be very patient, and you must increase your times and distances in very small increments. Finally, practice with the dog on a lead by the front door or in the car. For a reward, take him for a walk!

Tip: Don't stare at your dog during the *stay*. This is perceived by the dog as a threat and often intimidates the dog, causing it to squirm out of position or to creep to you submissively.

Come: Coming on command is more than a cute trick; it could save your dog's life. Your puppy probably already knows how to come. After all, it comes when it sees you with the food bowl or perhaps with the leash or a favorite toy. You may have even used the word come to get its attention then; if so, you have a head start. You want your puppy to respond to "Beanie, Come" with the same enthusiasm it would have if you were setting down his supper; in other words, *come* should always be associated with good things.

Sighthounds are notorious for not coming on command. The Whippet is not the average sighthound in this respect, being quite willing to come flying at the hint of a invitation. Still, don't expect your Whippet to do this reliably without a good training background. Just because your Whippet seems eager to come at home, take the time to train it to come under any condition.

Think about what excites your Whippet and makes it run to you. For most young Whippets, the opportunity to chase after you is one of the grandest games ever invented. Of course, most young Whippets will jump at the chance to gobble up a special treat. Combine these two urges, and use them to entice your Whippet to come on the run.

The best time to start is when your Whippet is a young puppy, but it is never too late. You will need a helper and an enclosed area. A hallway is perfect for a very young pup. Have your helper gently restrain the puppy while you back away and entice the puppy. Do whatever it takes at first: ask the pup if it wants a cookie, wave a treat or favorite toy, even crawl on

your hands and knees. The point is to get the pup's attention and to get it struggling to get away and get to you. Only at this point should you call out

Start teaching your puppy to come by having a helper prevent it from coming at first. Only after it is struggling to get to you (and your treats) should the helper give in and let the puppy run to you.

Food can be used to teach all sorts of tricks.

"Beanie, Come!" with great enthusiasm at the same time turning around and running away. Your helper will release the pup at the same time, and you should let it catch up to you. Reward it by playing for a second, then kneel down and give it the special treat. Repeat this several times a day, gradually increasing the distance, taking care never to practice past the time when your pup begins to tire of the game. Always keep a jolly attitude, and make the pup feel lucky to be part of such a wonderful game.

Once your puppy has learned the meaning of *come*, move your training outdoors. With the pup on a lead, command "Beanie, Come!" enthusiastically and quickly run away. When he reaches you, praise and reward! If he ignores you for more than a second, tug on the lead to get the pup's attention, but do not drag the puppy. Response to the *come* command is not one that can be put off until your dog feels like coming. In addition, the longer you separate the tug from the command, the harder it will be for your pup to relate the two, and in the long run, the harder the training will be on the youngster. After the tug, be sure to run backward and make the pup think that it was all part of the grand game.

Next, attach a longer line to the pup, allow it to meander about, and in the midst of its investigations, call, run backward, and reward. After a few repetitions, drop the long line, let your Whippet mosey around a bit, then call. If it begins to come, run away and let it chase you as part of the game. If your dog doesn't come, pick up the line and give a tug, then run away as usual. If at any time your Whippet runs the other way, never chase it. Chase the line, not the dog. The only game a Whippet likes more than chasing you is being chased by you. It will always win. Chase the line, grab it, give a tug, then run the other way.

Whippets use their ears to convey their mood and interest.

As your dog becomes more reliable, you should begin to practice (still on the long line) in the presence of distractions, such as other leashed dogs, unfamiliar people, cats, and cars. In most of these cases, you should not let the dog drag the line but hold on just in case the distractions prove too enticing.

Some dogs develop a habit of dancing around just out of reach of you, considering your futile grabs to be another part of this wonderful game. You can prevent this by requiring your dog to allow you to hold it by the collar before you reward it. Eventually, you may add sitting in front of you as part of the game.

This may seem like a lot of work, but it will save you a lot of wasted time in the long run and perhaps a lot of grief. Besides, it should be fun, not work!

Tip: Never have your dog come to you and then scold it for something it has done. In the dog's mind, it is being scolded for coming, not for any earlier misdeed. You should not call your dog to you at the end of an off-lead walk. You don't want the dog to associate coming to you with relinquishing its freedom. Call it to you several times during the walk, reward and praise it, and then send it back out to play.

Down: When you need your Whippet to stay in one place for a long time, it is best for it to be left in a *down/stay.* Begin teaching the *down* command with the dog in the sitting position. Command "*Beanie, Down,*" then show him a tidbit, and move it below his nose toward the ground. If he reaches down to get it, give it to him. Repeat, requiring him to reach further down (without lifting his rear from the ground) until he has to lower his elbows to the ground. Never try to cram your dog into the *down* position, which can scare a submissive dog

and cause a dominant dog to resist. Practice the *down/stay* just as you did the *sit/stay.*

Tip: Whippets don't mind learning the *down,* but they do mind having to lie on a cold, hard floor. Initial training will be much easier if you do it on a soft, warm surface.

Heel: Walking alongside of you on a lead may be a new experience for a youngster, and many will freeze in their tracks once they discover their freedom is being violated. In this case, do not simply drag the pup along, but coax it with food. When the puppy follows you, praise and reward. In this way, the pup comes to realize that following you while walking on a lead pays off.

Some Whippets have a tendency to forge ahead, pulling their hapless owners behind them in pursuit of every squirrel in sight. Although at times this may be acceptable to you, at other times it will be annoying and

Once the sit *is mastered, use food to lure your dog to the* down *position. You may have to keep a hand on its rump to prevent it from getting up.*

Don't jerk your dog into heel *position. Guide it with food. Proper* heel *position is on your left side, with the dog's neck in line with your leg.*

perhaps even dangerous. Even if you have no intention of teaching a perfect competition *heel*, you need to teach *heel* as a way of letting your Whippet know it is your turn to be the leader.

Have your Whippet sit in *heel* position; that is, on your left side with its neck next to and parallel with your leg. Say "*Beanie, Heel*," and step off with your left foot first. Remember that you stepped off on your right foot when you left your dog on a *stay*; if you are consistent, the foot that moves first will provide an eye level cue for your dog. During your first few practice sessions, you will keep him on a short lead, holding him in *heel* position, and of course, praising him. The traditional method of letting the dog lunge to the end of the lead and then snapping it back is unfair if you haven't first shown

the dog what is expected. Instead, after a few sessions of showing the dog *heel* position, give him a little more loose lead, and use a tidbit to guide him into correct position. If your Whippet still forges ahead after you have shown it what is expected, pull your dog back to position with a quick, gentle tug, then release, of the lead. If after a few days' practice, your dog still seems oblivious to your efforts, then turn unexpectedly several times; teach your dog that it must keep an eye on you. Keep in mind that every time you do this, you cause your Whippet to heel a little bit farther back in relation to you. In the long run, more Whippets have a problem with lagging way behind than with forging ahead. In other words, don't go overboard when trying to correct forging. It will tend to self correct with just a little guidance.

As you progress, you will want to add some *right*, *left*, and *about-faces* and to walk at all different speeds. Practice in different areas (still always on lead) and around different distractions. You can teach your Whippet to sit every time you stop. Vary your routine to combat boredom, and keep training sessions short. Be sure to give the *OK!* command before allowing your dog to sniff, forge, and meander on lead.

Tip: Keep a pace that requires your Whippet to walk fairly briskly. Too slow a pace gives your dog time to sniff, look all around, and in general, become distracted. A brisk pace will focus the dog's attention upon you and generally aid training.

Tricks and treats: The only problem with basic obedience skills is that they don't exactly astound your friends. For that you need something flashy, some incredible feat of intelligence and dexterity: a dog trick. Try the standards: *roll over*, *play dead*, *catch*, *sit up*, *speak*. All are easy to teach with the help of the same obedience concepts outlined in the training section. Teach *speak* by saying *"Speak"* when it appears your Whippet is about to bark. If your dog can physically do it, you can teach your dog when to do it.

The Whippet's World

Despite being dubbed *man's best friend*, the relationship between human and dog is a one-sided one. People expect their dogs to understand them, seldom bothering to try to learn the dog's language. With very little effort, you can meet your Whippet half way and learn to speak Whippet-ese.

Living with a Whippet is like having a wolf in the house—sort of. As much as they have shaken off their wild vestiges, Whippets still speak the ancestral language of wolves.
• A wagging tail and lowered head upon greeting are signs of submission.
• A lowered body, wagging and tucked tail, urination, and perhaps even rolling over are signs of extreme submission.
• A yawn is often a sign of nervousness. Drooling and panting can indicate extreme nervousness (as well as car sickness).
• Exposed teeth, a high and rigidly held tail, raised hackles, very upright posture, stiff-legged gait, and direct stare indicate very dominant behavior.
• A wagging tail, front legs and elbows on the ground, and rear in the air indicate the classic *play-bow* position and are an invitation for a game.

A dominant Whippet exhibits a classic threatening posture, which the submissive Whippet responds to with submissive body language.

The classic play-bow *position.*

The Worldly Whippet

Half the fun of owning an exotic and athletic dog is showing it off in public and including it in outdoor adventures. Half the problem of owning such a dog is that you attract attention wherever you go. People stop to ask about your dog and can't resist petting it.

While this can be a great deal of fun and a wonderful way to meet people, it won't be much fun if your Whippet is snarling, cowering, or jumping all over everyone it meets. Your Whippet must behave as a good citizen in public if it is to leave people with a good impression.

Citizen Canine

In order to recognize dogs formally that behave in public, the AKC offers the Canine Good Citizen (CGC) certificate, which requires your Whippet to:
• Accept a friendly stranger who greets you.
• Sit politely for petting by a stranger.
• Allow a stranger to pet and groom it.
• Walk politely on a loose lead.
• Walk through a crowd on a lead.
• *Sit* and *lie down* on command and *stay* while on a 20-foot (6 m) line.
• Calm down after play.
• React politely to another dog. React calmly to distractions.
• Remain calmly when tied for three minutes in the owner's absence, under supervision by a stranger.

The CGC is perhaps the most important title your Whippet can earn. The most magnificent champion in the show or obedience ring is no credit to its breed if it is not a good public citizen in the real world. Remember, to be a dog-owning good citizen yourself:
• Always clean up after your dog. Carry a plastic bag for disposal later.
• Don't let your dog run loose where it could bother picnickers, bicyclists, joggers, or children.
• Never let your dog bark unchecked.
• Never let your dog jump up on people.

Rapid Transit

Whippets make excellent travel companions. They are small enough to fit handily into any car yet large enough to share most outdoor adventures along the way. A dog gives you a good excuse to stop and enjoy the scenery up close and maybe even get some exercise along the way. With proper planning, you will find that a

The reflection of perfection. A worldly whippet acts as lovely as it looks.

Your Whippet will enjoy nature excursions, but make sure dogs are allowed before trekking to a distant locale. Many beaches, for example, do not allow dogs—yet the beach is Whippet paradise!

Whippet copilot can steer you to destinations you might otherwise have passed.

Without proper planning, sharing your trip with any dog can be a nightmare as you are turned away from motels, parks, attractions, and beaches. It's no fun trying to sneak a dog into a motel room; Whippets are just a tad too big to fit under your coat; besides, the mutest Whippet will find plenty to bark at once it discovers you're trying to keep it quiet! Several books are available listing establishments that accept pets. Call ahead to attractions to see if they have safe boarding arrangements for pets.

The number of establishments that accept pets decreases yearly. You can thank dog owners who seem to think their little Poopsie is above the law, owners who let Poopsie poop on sidewalks, beaches, and playgrounds, bark herself hoarse in the motel room, and leave behind wet spots on the carpet and chew marks on the chairs. Miraculously, some places still welcome pets. Please do everything you can to convince motel managers that dogs can be civilized guests.

Whether you will be spending your nights at a motel, campground, or even a friend's home, always have your dog on its very best behavior. Ask beforehand if it will be OK for you to bring your Whippet. Have your dog clean and parasite-free. Do not allow your dog to run helter-skelter through the homes of friends. Bring your dog's own clean blanket or bed, or better yet, its cage. Your Whippet will appreciate the familiar place to sleep, and your

A secured cage is the doggy equivalent of a seat belt.

out the window for a big whiff of country air. However, you are smarter than your Whippet (at least in this matter) and know that it should always ride in the equivalent of a doggy seat belt: the cage. Not only can a cage help to prevent accidents by keeping your dog from using your lap as a trampoline, but if an accident does happen, a cage can save your dog's life. A cage with a padlocked door can also be useful when you need to leave the dog in the car with the windows down.

Always walk your Whippet on lead when away from home. If frightened or distracted, your dog could become disoriented and lost. The long, retractable leads are ideal for traveling. Keep an eye out for little nature excursions, which are wonderful for refreshing both dog and owner. However, always do so with a cautious eye; never risk your dog's safety, or your own, by stopping in totally desolate locales, no matter how breathtaking the view.

Don't forget to pack:
• heartworm preventive and any other medications, especially antidiarrheal medication
• food and water bowls
• food, dog biscuits, and chewies
• bottled water or water from home—many dogs are very sensitive to changes in water and can develop diarrhea
• flea comb and brush
• moist towelettes, paper towels, and self-rinse shampoo
• bedding
• short and long leashes
• sweater for cold weather
• flashlight for night walks
• plastic baggies or other poop disposal means
• license tags, including a tag indicating where you could be reached while on your trip or the address of someone you know will be at home
• health and rabies certificates

friends and motel owners will breathe sighs of relief. Even though your dog may be accustomed to sleeping on furniture at home, a proper canine guest stays off the furniture when visiting. However, most Whippets are adept at looking sufficiently pitiful that your host will usually tell you to get out of the chair and let your dog into it! Walk and walk your dog (and clean up after it) to make sure no accidents occur inside. If they do, clean them immediately. Don't leave any surprises for your hosts! Changes in water or food, or simply stress, can often result in diarrhea, so be particularly attentive to taking your dog out often.

Never leave your dog unattended in a strange place. The dog's perception is that you have left and forgotten it. It either barks and tries to dig its way out through the doors and windows in an effort to find you or becomes upset and relieves itself on the carpet. Always remember that anyone who allows your dog to spend the night is doing so with a certain amount of trepidation; make sure they invite both of you back.

By car: When in the car, your Whippet will want to cuddle in your lap or close by your side, or hang its head

• recent color photo in case your Whippet somehow gets lost

By air: Air travel is fairly safe but should not be undertaken frivolously. Although air compartments are heated, they are not air-conditioned, and in hot weather, dogs have been known to overheat while the plane was still on the runway. Never travel during the heat of day. It's best if your dog can fly as excess baggage. If you must ship your Whippet by itself, ship counter-to-counter rather than as air freight. Make sure the cage is secure. For good measure, put an elastic *bungee* band around the cage door. Don't feed your dog before traveling. The night before the trip, fill a small bucket with water and freeze it. Take it out of the cooler just before the flight, and attach the bucket to the inside of the cage door with an eyebolt snap. As the ice melts during the flight, your dog will have water that otherwise might have spilled out during the loading process. Also include a large chewbone to occupy your jet-setter. Be sure to line the cage with soft, absorbent material, preferably something that can be thrown away if soiled.

With a little foresight, you may find your Whippet to be the most entertaining and enjoyable travel companion you could invite along. Don't be surprised if you find your dog nestled in your suitcase among your packed clothes!

Boarding: Sometimes you must leave your dog behind when you travel. Your dog may be more comfortable if an experienced pet sitter or responsible friend comes to your home to feed and exercise your dog regularly. This works best if you have a doggy door. The kid next door is seldom a good choice for this important responsibility. Unless the sitter is an experienced dog person, the dog may easily slip out the door or signs of illness may go unnoticed. The life of your dog is a heavy responsibility for a child.

Your Whippet may be safer (if not quite as contented) if you board it at a kennel. The ideal kennel will be approved by the American Boarding Kennel Association, have climate-controlled accommodations, and will keep your Whippet either indoors or in a combination indoor/outdoor run. Make an unannounced visit to the kennel, and ask to see the facilities. While you can't expect spotlessness and a perfumy atmosphere, most runs should be clean, and the odor should not be overwhelming. All dogs should have clean water and at least some dogs (including any Whippets!) should have soft bedding. Good kennels will require proof of immunizations and an incoming check for fleas. They will allow you to bring toys and bedding, and will administer prescribed medication. Strange dogs should not be allowed to mingle, and the entire kennel area should be fenced.

Whatever means you choose, always leave emergency numbers and your veterinarian's name. Make arrangements with your veterinarian to treat your dog for any problems that may arise. This means leaving a written agreement stating that you give permission for treatment and accept responsibility for charges.

Lost and Found

Whippets usually stick pretty close, but sometimes the unforeseeable happens, and you and your dog are suddenly separated. If so, you need to act quickly. Don't rely on the dog's fabled ability to find its way home. Whippets don't seem to be overly gifted in this area.

Start your search at the very worst place you could imagine your dog going, usually the nearest road. Don't drive so recklessly that you endanger your own dog's life should it run

Whippets use their acute senses of smell, hearing, and vision to seek out game. If they find it, expect a chase, possibly leading to danger.

across the road. Next, get pictures of your dog and go door-to-door. Call the local animal control, police department, and veterinarians. Hang up large posters with a picture of your dog or a similar looking Whippet. Take out an ad in the local paper. Mention a reward, but do not specify an amount.

The strikingly exotic look of the Whippet makes it attractive to dognappers. Never leave your dog in a place where it could be taken. Some dognappers steal expensive-looking dogs so they can collect large rewards, but you should never give anyone reward money before seeing your dog. Some scam artists answer lost dog ads and ask for money to ship the dog back to you from a distance or to pay vet bills when they don't really have your dog.

If your dog is tattooed, you can have the person read the tattoo to you in order to identify it positively.

Even license tags cannot always ensure your dog's return, because they must be on the dog to be effective. Tattooing your social security number or your dog's registration number on the inside of its thigh provides a permanent means of identification; these numbers can be registered with one of the several lost pet recovery agencies. Microchips are available that are placed under the dog's skin with a simple injection. They contain information about the dog and cannot be removed but require a special scanner (owned by most animal shelters) to be read. You may wish to discuss this option with your veterinarian or local breeders.

Whippin' the Competition

It's impossible to own a Whippet without becoming enthralled by the vision of it standing at attention in the backyard or having your breath taken away by its dizzying speed. It's only natural to want to show off the apple of your eye. Proud owners have flaunted their Whippets in races, dog shows, and other contests for over a century. Whippets have, in turn, proven to be formidable competitors.

Two For the Show

With a curvaceous silhouette unsurpassed in terms of elegance and sleekness, the Whippet is a standout among all the dogs at a show. If you have visions of competing with your Whippet in conformation events, be forewarned that you are going to need a good one. If you plan to breed your Whippet, you are going to need a great one.

It may take a year or more to find a good show Whippet; part of this time will be spent learning the standard, studying the breed, and talking to breeders. It's best to get your show Whippet from a successful show breeder. A breeder who lives near you can help show you how to prepare your dog for the ring and give you tips on showing it. The *Whippet News* and the *Whippet News Annual* are both published by the American Whippet Club and will provide a good background of Whippet lines available. *Sighthound Review* magazine is devoted to all sighthounds, with an emphasis on Whippets, and will be a real asset in your quest.

As long as your Whippet is at least six months of age, AKC registered, is neither spayed nor neutered, (if male) has two normally descended testicles, and has no disqualifying faults (see the official standard, pages 91–93), it can be shown. Winning with your first show prospect is sometimes hard. However, you will still learn a lot about the show world and be better prepared in the event that you would like to show your next Whippet (of course you will have more than one!).

The show Whippet must trot easily about the ring and pose when stopped. The show pose is simply to stand with the front legs parallel to each other and perpendicular to the ground, and the back legs also parallel to each other but set wider than the front legs and with the hocks perpendicular to the ground. The head is held up and the tail is held down. It helps if your Whippet will *bait*, that is, look

Whippet judging.

Whippets are one of the easier breeds to show, and you should get the hang of it in fairly short order. Many outings will be needed, however before both you and your Whippet will give a polished performance. Professional handlers could show your dog for you and probably win more often than you would. However, there is nothing like the thrill of winning when you are on the other end of the lead!

Contact your local kennel club and find out if they have handling classes or when the next match will be held. Matches are informal events where everybody's learning: puppies, handlers, even the judges. Don't take either a win or a loss at a match too seriously. In fact, even at a regular show, remember that the results are just one judge's opinion.

At a real AKC show, each time a judge chooses your dog as the best dog of its sex if it is not already a Champion, your dog wins up to five points, depending upon how many dogs it defeats. To become an AKC Champion (Ch), your Whippet must wi 15 points including two majors (defeating enough dogs to win three to five points at a time) . You may enter any class for which your dog is eligible: Puppy, Novice, American Bred, Bred b Exhibitor, or Open. The Best of Breed class is for dogs that are already Chan pions. Before entering, you should con tact the AKC and ask for the free dog show regulation pamphlet, which will explain the requirements for each clas Your dog must be entered about three weeks before the show date, and you will need to get a premium list and ent form from the appropriate show superintendent. Superintendents' addresses are available from the AKC or most do magazines.

Because Whippets are so much a true family member, it can hurt to have your beloved dog placed last in its class. Just be sure that your

attentively at a little tidbit or toy. The show Whippet must be able to stand posed on a table without showing resentment or shyness when the judge touches it. The judge will examine each Whippet from head to tail and rank every dog according to its adherence to the official breed standard (see Appendix).

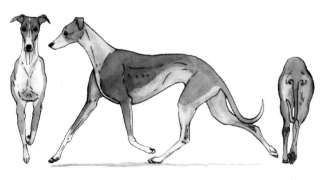

Show Whippets are evaluated both standing and trotting. When trotting, the judge looks for long, easy strides as viewed from the side, with legs that (with increasing speed) converge in a straight line toward the center of balance as viewed from the front and rear.

Whippet doesn't catch on, and always treat your dog like a Best in Show winner whether it gets a blue ribbon or no ribbon at all. To survive as a conformation competitor, you must be able to separate your own ego and self-esteem from your dog. You must also not allow your dog's ability to win in the ring cloud your perception of your dog's true worth in its primary role: that of friend and companion.

Mind Games

If your Whippet is more than just another pretty face, you may wish to enter an obedience trial, where your little gifted one can earn degrees attesting to its mastery of various levels of obedience. You and your Whippet will have to prove yourselves in front of a judge at three different obedience trials in order to have an obedience title officially become part of your dog's name.

You plan to teach your Whippet the commands *heel*, *sit*, *down*, *come*, and *stay* for use in everyday life. Add the command *stand for exam*, and your dog will have the basic skills necessary to earn the AKC Companion Dog (CD) title. The AKC will send you a free pamphlet describing obedience trial regulations.

Specifically, the AKC CD title requires the dog to:
• heel on lead, sitting automatically each time you stop, negotiating right, left, and about-turns without guidance from you, and changing to a faster and slower pace;
• heel in a figure eight around two people, still on lead;
• stand still off lead six feet (1.8 m) away from you and allow a judge to touch it;
• do the exercises described in the beginning of this list, except off lead;
• come to you when called from 20 feet (6 m) away and then return to heel position on command;

• stay in a sitting position with a group of other dogs, while you are 20 feet (6 m) away, for one minute;
• stay in a down position with the same group, while you are 20 feet (6 m) away, for three minutes.

Each exercise has points assigned to it, and points are deducted for the inevitable imperfections. No food can be carried into the ring. You must pass each individual exercise to qualify, and to earn the degree, you must qualify three times. The AKC will send a free rulebook to you on request.

Higher degrees of Companion Dog Excellent (CDX) or Utility Dog (UD) and Utility Dog Excellent (UDX) also require retrieving, jumping, hand signals, and scent discrimination. These advanced titles are rarely found in any sighthounds—except Whippets.

Dog obedience classes are often sponsored by obedience clubs and are a must if you plan to compete. Classes are a valuable source of training advice and encouragement from

Representing the breed in the hound group competition at the Westminster Dog Show is a great honor.

people who are experienced obedience competitors. They provide an environment filled with distractions similar to what you will encounter at an actual trial. Sit in on a class, and watch how the dogs are treated. If rough methods are used, look for another class.

The successful show Whippet is sound of body and mind, an elegant athlete that conforms to the standard and has that extra sparkle that commands attention.

If you enter competition with your Whippet, remember your golden rule: Companion Dog means just that, being upset at your dog because it made a mistake defeats the purpose of obedience as a way of promoting a harmonious partnership between trainer and dog. Failing a trial, in the scope of life, is an insignificant event. Never let a ribbon or a few points become more important than a trusting relationship with your companion. Besides, your Whippet will forgive you for the times you mess up!

Whippet Whiffers

A sighthound masquerading as a scenthound? No problem for a Whippet. Although it takes a little training, Whippets can be taught to use their noses and follow a track. The Tracking Dog (TD) title is earned by following a human trail about 500 yards (457 m) long that was laid up to two hours earlier. More advanced titles of Tracking Dog Excellent (TDX) and Variable Surface Tracker (VST) can also be earned.

Jumping For Joy

Not only are Whippets one of the fastest breeds around, but they also are one of the most agile. Whippets can jump, sprint, climb, balance, and weave with amazing nimbleness. The sport of agility allows them to hone their skills on an obstacle course of tunnels, seesaws, balance beams, jumps, and weave poles. The major problem with Whippets is trying to get them to control their excitement! The AKC awards, in increasing level of difficulty, the titles Novice Agility Dog (NAD), Open Agility Dog (OAD), Agility Dog Excellent (ADE), and Master Agility Excellent (MAX). The United States Dog Agility Association (USDAA) and United Kennel Club (UKC) also sponsor trials and award titles.

Many obedience clubs are now sponsoring agility training, but you can start some of the fundamentals at home. Entice your dog to walk through a tunnel made of sheets draped over chairs; guide it with treats to weave in and out of a series of poles made from several plumber's helpers placed in line; make it comfortable walking on a wide, raised board; teach your dog to jump through a tire and over a hurdle. If you can't find a club to train with, you can make your own equipment. Contact the AKC, USDAA, or UKC for regulations.

Flying For Frisbees

Many Whippet owners toss a Frisbee at their dogs, expecting that the dog will leap into the air and latch right on to it, only to have their dog duck and wince at the sight of the disk coming its way. Most dogs, Whippets included, have to be taught how fun Frisbee catching is. You don't teach them this by throwing a Frisbee at them, though. You start with little steps, with little dogs.

Start with your young Whippet by having it chase after a rag lure dragged across the ground. Let it catch the lure, then entice your Whippet back to you and praise lavishly. Next, encourage the pup to chase after and retrieve a ball. Rolling the ball so that it bounces back off of a wall tends to increase the pup's interest. When your Whippet is chasing and retrieving with gusto, it's time for the next step: catching. Again, start with the rag lure and pop it into the air as the pup chases it. Only allow the puppy to catch it in the air. Attach its ball to the lure, and encourage the puppy to catch it in the air. (You can partially split a tennis ball and tie it around the split part.) During this phase of training, you can also introduce the Frisbee. Roll the Frisbee along the ground, and praise your pup

Grooming for show takes only a little extra work. The scraggly hairs under the tail, at the rear of the thighs, and on the sides of the neck are carefully trimmed to give the dog a more clean-cut look.

for bringing it to you. Eventually, tie it to the lure, and have your pup snatch it from the air. Now comes the hard part: catching. Start with little dog treats thrown above your dog's nose. When the treat hits the floor, grab it before your dog can. Eventually, your dog will realize the only way it can get the treat is to catch it before it hits the ground. This step takes time, but your Whippet will figure it out if you are consistent. Once food catching is

Whippet Snippet: In 1974, a young man and his dog dashed onto the playing field at a nationally televised baseball game and regaled the audience with phenomenal Frisbee-catching feats before one of them (the man) was arrested, leaving the other one (the dog) running loose to be rescued by a fan. The display placed the sport of canine Frisbee in the public eye, and the dog thus became the most famous Whippet of all time: Ashley Whippet.

Few breeds are as suitably built for agility as the Whippet.

save the jumps and twirls until it is at least a year old.

Canine Frisbee contests can now be found all over the country, from local competitions to regional and national events. In freestyle competition, competitors are judged on their teamwork, originality, and athletic agility as they spin, twirl, and leap to great heights in pursuit of the flying disk. In mini-distance competition, the dog is scored on how many catches it makes in one minute, with scoring weighted by distance and height of the catch. Whippets continue to excel at the sport, but most Whippets do their high flying with only their owner and a few passersby to marvel at them. In larger cities, you may be able to find a dog disk club.

mastered, try a bouncing ball. Once that's mastered—the Frisbee. Be sure to use one of the soft disks especially made for dogs. They are much easier on a Whippet's delicate mouth. You can start training your dog to be a Frisbee freak when it is a puppy, but

Whippets are one of the most versatile breeds when it comes to competing successfully in a variety of fields. Despite this, most Whippets never step foot into a ring and never win a ribbon. They don't have to. They've already won the biggest prize of all— their owner's heart.

Fast Friends

Whippets long to cuddle, love to sleep, and like to eat. However, these all pale in comparison to Whippets' lust for speed. They like nothing better than for that speed to be admired by their special people.

Whippet owners do, indeed, find that watching their dogs race the wind evokes such feelings of admiration and aesthetic appreciation that it is one of the highlights of Whippet ownership. In fact, Whippeteers are so proud of their speedsters that they have arranged for their Whippets to compete in more varied running events than are available to any other breed of dog. Today Whippets can race more than the wind; they can race each other, the clock, or even real or imaginary bunnies, all in popular, competitive events.

A Racing Heart

In racing, a group of Whippets are all released from a box and are timed until they cross a finish line. Two types of Whippet racing are popular: straight and oval.

Straight Racing

No breed of dog can accelerate to such high speed in as little space and time as the Whippet. It was this phenomenal burst of speed that made Whippets so popular with the coal miners as poaching aids and betting objects. No expansive spaces, fancy enclosures, or special equipment was necessary in order to stage a Whippet race. All that was needed was someone to hold and then release (slip) the dog, and someone downfield to wave a rag to attract the dog. In the interest of fairness, today the slippers have been replaced by a starting box and the rag wavers by a lure, but the concept is essentially unchanged.

The American Whippet Club (AWC) sponsored National Point Racing (NPR) for years, awarding the coveted Award of Racing Merit (ARM). When the AWC withdrew from sponsoring racing in the mid-1990s, the Whippet Racing Association (WRA) stepped in, awarding the Whippet Race Champion (WRCh) title in place of the ARM. Still other races are sponsored by the North American Whippet Racing Association (NAWRA) and the Continental Whippet Association (CWA) awards the Racing Champion (RCH) title. CWA awards several titles, some of which require showring excellence in addition to racing excellence. In England, racing is sponsored by the Whippet Club Racing Association (WCRA), which awards the Whippet Club Racing Champion (WCRCh).

Races for adults are typically 200 yards (183 m) long, with those for puppies (eight to 13 months old) only 150 yards (138 m). Six Whippets compete in each race, and several races are run at each meet. Racers are graded according to their previous performances, with Grade A being reserved for the fastest.

Whippet Snippet: The record speed for a 200-yard (183 m) sprint is 10.8 seconds, an average speed of 38.5 miles per hour (62.1 km/hr).

They're off! It takes a little practice to perfect a fast break from the starting box.

Matching stride for stride, race winners are often measured in milliseconds.

Oval Racing

In the late 1930s and early 1940s, Whippets competed on a few commercial dog-racing tracks, but they never gained the popularity of Greyhounds as racers. Whippets thus avoided the massive commercial overbreeding that has been the bane of their cousin. With the Greyhound firmly entrenched as master of the track, there is no fear that the Whippet will ever follow in their pawsteps. Amateur Whippet oval racing has always had a few ardent followers, and in recent years, interest has mushroomed.

The oval track is actually U-shaped, so some people refer to this type of racing as *U-val* instead of oval. Distances are longer than those in straight racing, averaging 385 yards (353 m). Dogs run in groups of four, with the same grade classes as for straight races. Unlike straight racers, dogs with breed disqualifications are eligible to compete in oval racing. The National Oval Track Racing Association (NOTRA) is the major sponsor of oval racing; it awards the Oval Racing Championship (CRC) and the Supreme CRC (SORC)

Racing preparation: Racing Whippets are every bit as specialized as are show Whippets. Thus, even though all Whippets will have a blast blasting down the track, if your dream is to compete in Grade A, you will need to find a dog from Grade A stock.

The best dog will never live up to its potential without the best of nutrition, conditioning, and training. Race dogs are never fat! They need ample protein with which to build muscles and ample exercise to turn that protein into muscles. Exercise should consist of both long walks and short sprints.

Training to chase the lure is started with the pole lure (see page 55). In addition, dogs must learn to tolerate a racing muzzle. This is usually readily accepted if combined with the fun of chasing. Let the dog catch the lure and immediately pull the muzzle off so that it can grab the lure. The greater challenge is training the dog to break from the starting box. Start at home by walking your pup through a cardboard box. String the lure through it, and practice letting your pup chase the lure through the box. Now loosely close the flap on the far end of the box, and pull the lure through it. Raise the flap as the pup approaches. Gradually make your pup wait longer for the flap to be opened, and reward it with a frolic after the lure. Don't let your pup cheat by going around the box! Eventually, you will need access to a real box and lure, but this at-home training will give your dog a good head start.

On Course

Coursing differs from racing in that it entails more than simply speed. The fastest of dogs is of little practical value if it cannot control that speed enough to turn after a hare or can only sustain that speed for a few feet. Thus, coursing entails the subjective judging of a dog's speed, agility, and endurance, as well as some other attributes depending upon whether it is open field coursing or lure coursing.

Open Field Coursing

While the Whippet was busy gathering food for the pot or providing entertainment for the betting miners, its rich cousin the Greyhound was also earning its keep by running game for the entertainment of gentry and noblemen. The sport of coursing, wherein the Greyhounds were loosed after hare, was so popular that it became known as the *sport of queens*, in part because of Queen Elizabeth I's interest in and influence upon the sport. To this day, coursing of hare by sighthounds retains

Straw hurdles are sometimes included in European races.

Young Whippets need very little incentive to chase and catch a soft lure.

In both open field and lure coursing, the slip lead allows the dog to be released instantly (by letting go of the loop in the right hand).

a keen following, although one need no longer be of the nobility to partake.

In Europe, the quarry is the European hare, while in America, it is the jackrabbit (actually a hare). Because jackrabbits are found only in the western areas of the United States, most organized open field coursing takes place in the desert regions of California. The Whippet's small size puts it at a disadvantage in the harsh desert terrain, and

some jacks can be almost as large as a Whippet. As a result, Whippet participation is limited compared with some of the other sighthound breeds. For those that do pass muster, the National Open Field Coursing Association (NOFCA) awards the titles of Coursing Champion (CC) for points won in competition with other sighthounds and Courser of Merit (CM) for points won in competition only with other Whippets. The North American Coursing Association (NACA) also sponsors hunts and awards NACC and NACM titles, comparable to the CC and CM.

Open field coursing requires a tough and committed dog and owner, entails some dangers, and often ends in the death of the quarry. For people who find these aspects unacceptable, the sport of lure coursing provides a fun, safe alternative.

Lure Coursing

By far the most popular Whippet sport, lure coursing is a simulated course wherein a lure (actually a common, white, plastic garbage bag) is dragged at high speeds around a predetermined path by means of a system of pulleys. Dogs run in groups of two or three and are scored on their speed, agility, endurance, enthusiasm, and follow. (Some smart alecks try to outsmart the lure and cut it off at the pass!)

Although all sighthound breeds are eligible to compete at lure-coursing trials, probably 80 percent of all entries are Whippets. Not only is this because Whippets are one of the most popular sighthound breeds, but they are also undeniably the best lure-coursing breed. In many breeds, the dogs are apt to try to play with one another or simply lose interest in the middle of the course. In contrast, it is a rare Whippet that does not run with single-minded intensity from start to finish, oblivious to the presence of its running mates. Good running Whippets have

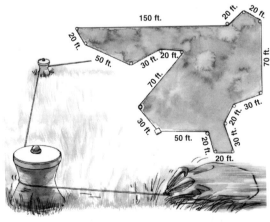

Layout for lure-coursing competition.

come from show-, racing-, and even pet-quality backgrounds, but the very best tend to come from backgrounds full of lure-coursing stars.

Even Whippets that have never seen a lure or a rabbit often go berserk at the sight of the lure speeding around the field. So if you are attending your first trial, a word of warning: hold on tight! Whippets are notorious for their wild antics as spectators. They jump straight up in the air on spring-loaded legs, all the while shrieking, "My turn, my turn!" in Whippet-ese.

The pole lure provides practice, exercise, and mostly—fun.

The pole lure: If you don't believe your little angel would deign to chase a fake rabbit, try this little experiment at home. Take a pole about six feet (1.8 m) long, and attach a string of about the same length to it. On the end of the string attach a lure, either the official plastic garbage bag, a white rag, or a scrap of fake (or real) fur. Now run around your backyard, whipping the lure around erratically. Let your dog watch from the other side of a fence or have someone hold it at first. Then, after your Whippet has been whipped to a frenzy, let it loose and watch the fun begin. Don't let your dog jump too crazily, though. You don't want it to hurt itself in its enthusiasm. Let your dog catch the lure occasionally, but don't let it be too easy, and always quit with your dog wanting more. The pole lure is an excellent training device for lure coursing but also makes a wonderful game and exercise device for everyday use.

Titles: Both the American Kennel Club (AKC) and the American Sighthound Field Association (ASFA) sponsor lure-coursing field trials and award titles. The AKC awards the suffix Junior Courser (JC) for a dog that demonstrates it can finish a course running by itself, the suffix Senior Courser (SC) for a dog that then demonstrates it can complete a course running alongside two other dogs, and

the prefix Field Champion (FC) for dogs that win against competition in a number of trials. The ASFA also awards a Field Champion (FCH) title, but as a suffix, for dogs that win over several trials against competition. The ASFA goes on to award the extremely competitive Lure Courser of Merit (LCM) suffix for continued success against other Field Champions. The ASFA holds more trials than the AKC at this time, but your Whippet will be equally elated at the chance to attend a trial sponsored by either organization. Contact either the AKC or the ASFA, and request a rule book and list of clubs and trials in your area.

The well-dressed Whippet: Bring a coat or sweater in cool weather for your dog to wear while it is warming up and

Whippet Snippet: To earn the LCM title, a dog must win 300 points and four first placements in the Field Champion stake—an extremely difficult feat. Some talented dogs have even earned twice the required points and placements, and have thus been awarded the title LCM 2. Two whippets have earned the amazing title of LCM14: FC Finghin's Wandering Joe and FC Carbeth Loud and Clear!

Lure coursers run in trios, each contender wearing an identifying yellow, pink, or blue blanket.

again after it has cooled down. In warm weather, bring water in which to soak your dog after running. A terry cloth jacket (made from a towel) can be soaked in water to serve as a cooling blanket on very hot days. Your Whippet will wear a lightweight coursing blanket while competing (you can borrow one at the trial). Some people will muzzle their dogs, not usually because they bite but because they catch the lure at the end of the course and won't let go! A muzzle can provide a sort of mouth guard, as well, in the event that the lure should ever get caught on a pulley and

"When is it going to be my turn?"

the dog inadvertently hit the pulley when trying to grab the lure. Many Whippets run with their front pasterns wrapped in Vet-Wrap (a miracle leg wrap that clings to itself and can be found at most horse supply stores, some pet stores, and veterinary clinics). At full speed, the rear of the pastern actually contacts the ground and is often abraded or bruised as a result. The large pad of the foot can also be peeled away, a painful but self-healing condition that can also be thwarted by wrapping. Ask other Whippet owners to help you get your dog ready. They will be happy to help you as much as possible because lure-coursing aficionados are always eager to encourage more to join their ranks!

Running safety: Some owners are reluctant to try racing or coursing because they fear their dog could be injured. True, any time your dog is active a certain risk is involved. However, (with the exception of open field coursing) the risks are minimal as long as your dog is in proper condition. Do not course or race your Whippet if it does not get regular conditioning by running during the week. If your dog has a previous injury, check with your veterinarian to make sure you don't risk reinjuring it. Remember, there is no such thing as halfway for a Whippet. Once you let it loose after the lure, it will not run at half speed or run half the distance. Make sure your dog is physically fit and sound or do not run your dog at all. Always limber your dog before running, and walk it afterward. If you expect to compete with your dog in an athletic event, be sure to treat it like the athlete it is.

At a lure-coursing trial, your Whippet will be required to run at least two runs (*courses*) in order to qualify, perhaps more in the event of ties or if it wins and goes on to compete for Best of Breed, and ultimately, Best in Field. Especially with an inexperienced dog, however, you should quit at any time your dog appears tired, overheated, sore, or lame.

Most courses are laid out in clear fields without obstructions, but some are laid out on hillsides or in the vicinity of trees. On hilly terrain, the string that runs along the course may be raised off the ground several inches. Heights greater than six inches are unacceptable when running a Whippet, as the dog can trip over it or be cut by the string running alongside its body. Inexperienced Whippets often overshoot turns, and if a tree is in the way, dogs could run into it while their attention is on the lure. It is the responsibility of the club to design a course that is safe for all dogs, but it is ultimately your responsibility to express any safety concerns you may have. The two problems described earlier can be easily alleviated by means of adding or moving pulleys. If your safety concerns are not met, pull your dog from competition and go home. The number one priority at any field trial should be safety.

Any kind of running activity is certainly more dangerous than snoozing on the couch, but everything worth

The ideal running area is wild, wonderful, and fenced.

doing in life comes with some risk. Is coursing worth doing? Ask the people that drive hundreds of miles every weekend to stand in the rain and watch their Whippet run a course, even though they know their dog may have little chance of winning. They do it because they enjoy watching a beautiful animal do what it does best, and because they enjoy watching their pet derive so much happiness. See for yourself: take your Whippet to a lure course and see what it says—if you can calm it down enough!

Whippet Sense: Sighthound Sight

It is often assumed that sighthounds have superior vision to other dogs, but in fact, the question is still up in the air. The Whippet certainly does have keen vision and very healthy eyes compared with other breeds. The canine eye is superior to the human eye at seeing in very dim light. This ability comes, in part, from a reflective structure (the tapetum lucidum) in the back of the eye that reflects light back into the light-sensitive cells of the retina, in essence magnifying the light. The reflected light is the eye shine you may see from your Whippet's eyes at night when you shine a light into them. The dog's ability to see in dim light is also due in part to it having a much greater proportion of retinal rod cells (which are highly sensitive to dim light) than do humans.

The price the dog pays for this night vision is the sacrifice of keen detail and color vision. The dog senses color like a color-blind person does. Neither is really blind to color at all. That is, each confuses similar shades of yellow-green, yellow, orange, and red but can readily see and discriminate blue, indigo, and violet from all other colors and from each other.

HOW-TO:
Quick Fixes (Coping With Running Injuries)

Whippets live to run, and they propel their bodies at speeds far too fast to be safe. Their legs move at an even faster rate, and it seems incredible that they get as few running injuries as they do. However, expect your Whippet to one day pull up on three legs.

Whippets occasionally take a tumble but usually come up unscathed. Still, in cases of collision or other serious accidents, you should stop your dog from running and take it home for observation.

The Whippet skeleton and musculature.

Immobilize a long bone fracture by wrapping it with a magazine and securing the magazine in place with Vet-Wrap or tape. Do not try to set the bone.

Limping may or may not indicate a serious problem. *Mild* lameness should be treated with complete rest; if it still persists after three days, your dog will need to be examined by its veterinarian. Ice packs (a frozen bag of vegetables works well) may help minimize swelling if applied immediately after an injury.

Fractures: Any time a dog is lame and also exhibits swelling or deformation of the affected leg, extreme pain, or grinding or popping sounds, a break or another serious problem could be indicated. Fractures should be immobilized by splinting above and below the site of fracture (a rolled magazine can work well on legs in an emergency) before moving the dog. It is imperative that the fractured area not be further traumatized by attempts to immobilize it; if in doubt, leave it alone. Regardless, immediate veterinary attention is required.

Feet and toes: If a toe is swollen, does not match its fellow on the opposite foot in shape and position, or makes a grinding sound when moved, or if the dog is in considerable pain, the toe should be immobilized and checked by your veterinarian. Meanwhile, minimize swelling by applying cold packs or placing the foot in a bucket of cold water.

Examine the feet of a lame dog for burrs, cuts, peeled pads, or misaligned toes. Split or broken nails can be treated by cutting the nail as short as possible and soaking it in warm salt water. Apply an antibiotic and then a human fingernail mender, followed by a bandage.

Cuts and peeled pads should be carefully flushed with warm water, and an antibacterial ointment should be applied. Cover the area with gauze, then wrap the foot with Vet-Wrap (a stretchable bandage that clings to itself). You can also add padding. Change the dressing twice daily (or anytime it gets wet), and restrict exercise until

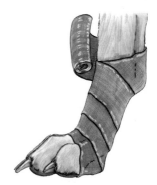

One method of wrapping an injured foot is to begin near the toes with the Vet-Wrap wrapping around the leg at a 45 degree angle to the ground so that it crosses over itself and clings better. Use a strip of adhesive tape to anchor its position at the top and bottom.

the foot heals. If you need a quick fix for a minor injury, you can fashion a makeshift pad by adhering a thin piece of rubber or leather to the bottom of the pad with superglue. You can also apply a coat of Nu-Skin (available at drug stores) if the injury is not too extensive. Peeled pads are very painful. A local anesthetic such as hemorrhoid cream or a topical toothache salve can help ease some of the discomfort. Deep cuts or extensive peeling should be checked by your veterinarian for foreign objects or tendon damage.

If the webbing between the toes is split, it will continue to split further. This is another condition that warrants a trip to the vet.

A deep cut directly above and behind the foot may sever the ligaments to the toes, causing them to lose their arch. Immediate veterinary attention should be sought, but even that may not help.

A *jammed toe* results from stubbing a toe on a root, rock, or other hard surface. A toe that is simply bruised will improve with rest, but any toe injury is potentially serious.

A displaced toe will stick out to the side, and the dog will be in extreme pain. Pull the toe gently forward, and allow it to go back into its proper position. Wrap the foot in Vet-Wrap, and seek veterinary attention. Toes that become dislocated often have stretched or torn ligaments, and the problem will tend to recur and worsen with each subsequent dislocation. An extended rest is mandatory.

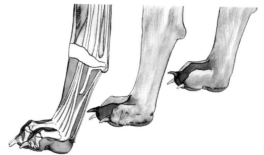

Normal toe placement, a dropped toe (due to tearing of the superficial digital flexor tendon), and a knocked up toe (due to tearing of the deep digital flexor tendon). These tendons are located in the rear of the pastern or hock.

Keeping the nail of the affected toe trimmed as short as possible may help as will wrapping the foot in Vet-Wrap before running and avoiding running on hard surfaces.

Knee injuries: Knee injuries, especially of the cruciate ligaments, are common in dogs, especially overweight dogs. They can also arise when the dog is pushed sideways while running. Most cruciate tears do not get well on their own. Still, cruciate surgery requires a commitment to careful nursing and should not be undertaken casually.

Muscle injuries: The most common nonfoot injuries are muscle injuries. These usually cause little lameness but pronounced swelling or can be felt as an indentation in a muscle. Torn muscles may need surgery for a complete recovery. All muscle injuries should be treated with an initial ice pack followed by at least a week's rest.

Puppy problems: Puppies are especially susceptible to bone and joint injuries, and should never be allowed to jump from high places or run until exhausted. Persistent limping in puppies may result from one of several developmental bone problems and should be checked by the veterinarian. Both puppies and adults should be discouraged from romping on slippery floors that could cause them to lose their footing.

Older dogs: In older dogs or dogs with a previous injury, limping is often the result of osteoarthritis. Arthritis can be treated with aspirin but should be done so only under veterinary supervision. Do not use naxopren. Your veterinarian can prescribe drugs that may help greatly. Any time a young or middle-aged dog shows signs of arthritis, especially in a joint that has not been previously injured, the dog should be examined by its veterinarian.

Treatment: Aspirin or newer prescription medications may alleviate some of the discomfort of injuries, but never give them if your dog is on its way to surgery. If you administer pain medication, you must confine your dog; lack of pain could encourage it to use the injured limb, ultimately resulting in further injury.

Playing It Safe

You need not attend a racing or coursing event to experience one of the greatest joys of Whippet ownership—watching one of nature's most athletic creations cavorting at Mach speed. Although the Whippet is one of the most obedient of the sighthound breeds, it is a true sighthound at heart, which means that it was bred to chase first and ask questions later. Thus, you must choose with utmost care a safe place to run your dog.

Everybody thinks their dog is smart, trustworthy, and reliable off lead. They may be right—until the unpredictable occurs: another dog attacks or a cat runs underfoot. Whatever the reason, the trustworthy dog forgets itself for just a moment—and that's all the time needed to run in front of a car. Trust is wonderful, but careless or blind trust is deadly.

Never allow your Whippet to run loose in sight of traffic, even if that traffic is a mere speck in the distance. A Whippet can be lured by the sight of a rabbit or cat, or chased by a stray dog, and can travel a great distance in a short time. No matter how trustworthy your Whippet seems, always remember its sighthound heritage.

Never unhook the leash until you know everything about the area. Are there so many squirrels and rabbits that your Whippet may be lured farther and farther away? Deer are a grave danger, because they are irresistible to Whippets and can lead them on a merry chase that may end in tragedy. Watch for poisonous snakes, alligators, or animals that could attack your dog. Watch for small animals and dogs that your dog could attack. Look out for cliffs, roadways, and drainage culverts. Avoid wilderness areas during hunting season. In fact, by dressing your Whippet in a bright coursing jacket, you can both help protect it from nearsighted hunters and locate it more easily yourself.

Many people find an empty school yard fits the bill. If you use a school yard, be sure to use a pooper scooper diligently if you want to keep that privilege; no one wants children falling in dog waste on the playground.

You should never take your dog into an unfenced area unless it is reliable at coming on command. If your Whippet does get loose and refuses to return, however, *don't chase it!* Run away from it, and it is more likely to follow. Get in your car, and drive away from it. This usually gets a Whippet's attention. If this is not possible, entice it with a pole lure, food, or another dog. When you do get your dog back, even if it has taken an hour and you are furious, don't punish it. Take better care not to let your dog get loose, and train your Whippet to come for its own safety! (See page 35.)

Some areas simply have no safe place to let your Whippet run loose. You can still do a good job of exercising it on leash, however. Walking the dog is excellent low-impact exercise for both of you and is especially good for elderly or recovering dogs. If you pick a regular time of day for your walk, you will have your own personal fitness coach goading you off the couch like clockwork.

For a walk around the neighborhood, use a choke or martingale collar so that it cannot slip over your Whippet's head, a six-foot (2 m) nonchain leash, or a retractable leash. Retractable leashes are great for walks, but you must be especially vigilant when using them because dogs can still dart out into the path of traffic when on them. Keep an eye out for loose dogs and cats, and hold your dog close around stray animals and passing pedestrians.

Keep up a brisk pace, and gradually work up to longer distances. A Whippet should walk at least a half mile daily and would prefer to walk several miles. Jogging can also be fun for

...lder dogs especially enjoy walking. Most are sufficiently well-behaved to walk in a group.

...our Whippet, but you must gradually ...ork up to longer distances and avoid ...ot weather. Dogs can't cool them-...elves as well as humans can, and ...eatstroke has taken the lives of far ...o many jogging dogs. Check the foot ...ads regularly for abrasions, gravel, ...aring, or blistering from hot pave-...ent. In winter, check between the ...ads for balls of ice, and rinse the feet ...hen returning from walking on rock ...alt. Finally, never jog, jump, or ...verexert a puppy. Their bones can ...e overstressed and damaged. Let a ...up run until it's tired but no more.

...Although being lazy and jogging your ...og beside a bicycle or car is tempting, ...ese are dangerous practices. It's too ...asy for your dog to see a cat or squir-...l and either pull you over or run into your path. If you do elect to try the lazy way out, despite warnings, you must train your dog to understand *heel* before starting and have your dog in *heel* position (except farther out from you) when on the move.

Whippets are elegant additions to any home, but they are more than decorative accessories. Whippets are finely tuned athletes awaiting their chance to push themselves to the limit and drink in the wind. Do your best to give them this chance, but as the sen-sible half of the partnership, don't take chances with safety. Besides, whether walking, jogging, or running, your Whippet will most relish the chance to simply share any adventure, no matter how wild or sedate, with its favorite person—you!

Bone Appetit!

The Whippet's lithe silhouette, as well as its condition, health, and ultimately, longevity, depend in part upon what you choose to set in front of it. One dizzying trip through the dog food section of a supermarket, pet supply store, or dog show vendor aisle will leave you utterly baffled and feeling like the worst dog owner ever created. Before you become paralyzed with indecision, keep in mind that dog nutritionists have done most of the work for you. As long as the food you choose passes some basic guidelines, it will be adequate to sustain your dog's life. It may not make your Whippet bloom with condition, however. For that, you do need to do a little investigating.

Look for the guaranteed analysis on every container of dog food to determine the protein and fat content; then examine the list of ingredients to see the source of these nutrients.

The Galloping Gourmet

Although dogs are members of the order carnivora ("meat-eaters"), they are actually omnivorous, meaning the nutritional needs can best be met by a diet derived from both animals and plants. Most dogs do have a decided preference for meat over nonmeat foods, but a balanced meal will combine both meat- and plant-based nutrients. These nutrients are commercially available in several forms. Most Whippet owners feed a combination of dry and canned food, supplemented with dog biscuits and possibly semimoist food.

Dry food (containing about 10 percent moisture) is the most popular, economical, and healthy. However, it is the least enticing form of dog food.

Semimoist food (with about 30 percent moisture) contains high levels of sugar used as preservatives. It is tasty, convenient, and very handy for traveling but is not an optimal nutritional choice as a regular diet. Pay no attention to the meatlike shapes; it starts out as a powder and is formed to look like meat chunks or ground beef.

Canned food has a high moisture content (about 75 percent), which helps to make it tasty. The high moisture content also makes it comparatively expensive, since you are in essence buying water. A steady diet of canned food would not provide the chewing necessary to maintain dental health. In addition, a high meat content tends to increase levels of dental plaque.

Chew sticks, nylon bones, dog biscuits, and carrots can help provide the chewing action necessary to rid dogs f some (but not all) dental plaque. The better varieties of dog biscuits provide complete nutrition. They are most commonly used as snacks or treats.

The Association of American Feed Control Officials (AAFCO) has recommended minimal nutrient levels for dogs based upon controlled feeding studies. Unless you are a nutritionist, the chance of you cooking up a homemade diet that meets these exacting standards is remote. So the first rule is to select a food that states on the label that it not only meets the requirements set by the AAFCO but also has been tested in *feeding trials.* You should also realize that when you add table scraps and other enticements, you are disrupting the balance of the diet.

Feed a high-quality food from a name brand company. Avoid food that has been sitting on the shelf for long periods, has holes in the bag, or has grease that has seeped through the bag. Always strive to buy and use only the freshest food available. Dry food loses nutrients as it sits, and the fat content can become rancid.

Shop around for a food that your Whippet enjoys. Mealtime is a highlight of a dog's day. Although a dog will eventually eat even the most unsavory of dog foods if given no choice, it hardly seems fair to deprive your family member of one of life's simple, and for a dog, most important, pleasures. Beware: dogs will often seem to prefer a new food when first offered, but this may simply be due to its novelty. Only after you buy a cupboard full of this alleged Whippet ambrosia will you discover it was just a passing fancy.

Boning Up on Nutrition

When comparing food labels, keep in mind that differences in moisture content make it difficult to make direct comparisons between the guaranteed analyses in different forms of food unless you first do some calculations

Whippet Sense: A Matter of Taste

Whippets have a discriminating sense of taste, as any owner knows who has tried to pawn off less than the best dog food on their Whippet. Dogs have most of the same taste receptors that we do, including similar sugar receptors (which explains why many have a sweet tooth). However, dogs do not perceive artificial sweeteners like we do; they seem to taste bitter to dogs. Research has shown that dogs, in general, prefer meat (not exactly earth-shaking news). While many individual differences exist, the average dog prefers beef, pork, lamb, chicken, and horse meat, in that order.

to equate the percentage of dry food matter. The components that vary most from one brand to another are protein and fat percentages.

Protein provides the necessary building blocks for growth and maintenance of bones, muscle, and coat and for the production of infection-fighting antibodies. The quality of protein is as important as the quantity of protein. Meat-derived protein is more highly digestible than plant-derived protein and is of higher quality. Most Whippets will do fine on regular adult foods having protein levels of about 20 percent (dry food percentage).

Fat is the calorie-rich component of foods, and most dogs prefer the taste of foods with higher fat content. Fat is necessary to good health by aiding in the transport of important vitamins and providing energy. Dogs deficient in fat often have sparse, dry coats.

Choose a food that has a protein and fat content best suited for your dog's life stage, adjusting for any weight or health problems (prescription diets formulated for specific health problems are available). Puppies and adolescents need

A Whippet in perfect condition has a smooth outline created from muscles, not fat.

"What's for supper?" Whippets tend to savor their meals, chewing carefully rather than gulping. Perhaps because they take the time to taste it, they have a reputation of being somewhat particular about what they eat.

particularly high protein and somewhat higher fat levels in their diets, such as the levels found in puppy foods. Stressed, highly active, or underweight dogs should be fed higher protein levels or even puppy food. Obese dogs or dogs with heart problems should be fed a lower-fat food. Older dogs, especially those with kidney problems, should be fed moderate levels of very high-quality protein. Studies have shown that high-protein diets do not cause kidney failure in older dogs. However, given a dog in which kidney stress or decompensation exists, a high-protein diet will do a lot of harm.

As important as the guaranteed analysis is the list of ingredients: a good rule of thumb is that three or four of the first six ingredients should be animal derived. These tend to be tastier and more highly digestible than plant-based ingredients; more highly digestible foods generally mean less stool volume and less gas problems.

You may have to do a little experimenting to find just the right food. A word of warning, though. One of the great mysteries of life is why a species such as the dog, that is renown for its lead stomach and preference to eat out of garbage cans, can, at the same time, develop violently upset stomachs simply by changing from one high-quality dog food to another. It happens. So when changing foods, you should do so gradually, mixing in progressively more and more of the new food each day for several days.

An Hourglass Figure

The dog's wild ancestor, the wolf, evolved to survive feast and famine, gorging following a kill but then perhaps waiting several days before another feast. In today's world, dogs can feast daily and without the period of famine, can easily become obese.

Many owners unaccustomed to the Whippet physique aren't satisfied until they have fattened it to nonWhippet dimensions. A Whippet in proper weight should have an hourglass figure whether viewed from above or the side. There should be no roll of fat over the withers or rump. The stomach should definitely be tucked up. The ribs should be easily felt through a thin layer of muscle. The Whippet is a sprinter and should have a sprinter's body: lean and muscular.

Overweight Whippets should be fed a high-fiber, low-fat and medium-protein diet dog food. Such commercially available diet foods, which supply about 15 percent fewer calories per pound, are preferable to the alternative of just feeding less of a fattening food.

Many people find that one of the many pleasures of dog ownership is sharing a special treat with their pet. Rather than giving up this bonding activity, substitute a low-calorie alternative such as rice cakes or carrots. Make sure family members aren't sneaking the dog forbidden tidbits. Keep the dog out of the kitchen or dining area at food preparation or meal times. Schedule a walk immediately following your dinner to get your dog's mind off of your leftovers—it will be good for both of you.

If your dog remains overweight, seek your veterinarian's opinion. Heart disease and some endocrine disorders, such as hypothyroidism, Cushing's disease, or the early stages of diabetes, can cause the appearance of obesity and should be ruled out or treated. However, most cases of obesity are simply from eating more calories than are expended. Obesity predisposes dogs to joint injuries and heart problems. The Whippet's long, slender legs were not meant to support a voluptuous torso. An obese Whippet cannot enjoy one its greatest pleasures in life—the ability to soar with the wind, skipping along like a windblown leaf—an ability that depends upon a svelte physique.

Athletic competitors need especially high quality protein.

Underweight Whippets may gain weight with puppy food; add water, milk, bouillon, or canned food, and heat slightly to increase aroma and palatability. Milk will cause many dogs to have diarrhea, so try only a little bit at first. Try a couple of dog food brands, but if your Whippet still won't

Mmmm, good. Whippets appreciate fine dining.

Whippet weight check: definite tuck up, easily felt (but not prominent) ribs and hipbones, an hourglass figure as viewed from above, no dimple where the tail meets the rump, no roll of fat over the withers.

eat, then you may have to employ some tough love. Many picky eaters are created when their owners begin to spice up their food with especially tasty treats. The dog then refuses to eat unless the preferred treat is offered and finally learns that if it refuses even that proffered treat, another even tastier enticement will be offered. Give your dog a good, tasty meal, but don't succumb to Whippet blackmail or you may be a slave to your dog's gastronomical whims for years to come.

Your veterinarian should examine your dog if its appetite fails to pick up or if it simply can't gain weight. Even more worrisome would be a dog that suddenly lost its appetite or weight. Such a problem can be a warning sign of a physical disorder.

A sick or recuperating dog may have to be coaxed into eating. Cat food or baby food containing meat are relished by dogs and may entice a dog without an appetite to eat.

Feeding schedules: Very young puppies should be fed three or four times a day on a regular schedule. Feed them as much as they care to eat in about 15 minutes. From the age of three to six months, pups should be fed three times daily and after that, twice daily. Adult dogs can be fed once a day, but it is actually preferable to feed smaller meals twice a day.

Some people let the dog decide when to eat by leaving food available at all times. If you choose to let the dog *self-feed*, monitor its weight to be sure it is not overindulging. Leave only dry food down. Canned food spoils rapidly and becomes both unsavory and unhealthy. If your dog overindulges, you will have to intervene before you have a roly-poly Whippet on your hands.

Water: Water is essential for your Whippet's health and comfort. Don't just keep your dog's water bowl full by topping it off every day. Such a habit allows algae to form along the sides of the bowl and gives bacteria a chance to multiply. Empty, scrub, and refill the water bowl daily. If the water bowl runs dry, your Whippet may turn to the toilet bowl as an alternative source. In fact, you should make it a practice to keep the lid down, because many dogs view the toilet bowl as an especially deluxe watering hole! It should go without saying that drinking from the toilet is not a healthy practice—and definitely not conducive to dog kisses!

Never feed:
- Chicken, pork, lamb, or fish bones. These can be swallowed, and their sharp ends can pierce the stomach or intestinal walls.
- Any bone that could be swallowed whole. This could cause choking or intestinal blockage.
- Any cooked bone. Cooked bones tend to break and splinter.
- Raw meat, which could contain salmonella.
- Mineral supplements unless advised to do so by your veterinarian.
- Chocolate. It contains theobromine, which is poisonous to dogs.
- Alcohol.

An Ounce of Prevention

An ounce of prevention really is worth a pound of cure. Preventive medicine encompasses accident prevention, vaccinations, parasite control, as well as good hygiene and grooming. It is a team effort directed by your veterinarian but undertaken by you. Choose your veterinarian carefully, and take your duties seriously.

The Well Whippet

The only way you will know if your Whippet may be sick is to become intimately in tune with it when it's well. Take five minutes weekly to perform a simple health check, examining:
- the mouth for red, bleeding, swollen, or pale gums, loose teeth, ulcers of the tongue or gums, or bad breath
- the eyes for discharge, cloudiness, or discolored whites
- the ears for foul odor, redness, or discharge
- the nose for thickened or colored discharge
- the skin for parasites, hair loss, crusts, red spots, or lumps
- the feet for cuts, abrasions, split nails, bumps, or misaligned toes

Observe your dog for signs of lameness or uncoordination, sore neck, circling, loss of muscling, and any behavioral change. Run your hands over the muscles and bones, and check that they are symmetrical from one side to the other. Weigh your dog, and observe whether it is putting on fat or wasting away. Check for any growths or swellings, which could indicate cancer or a number of less-serious problems. A sore that does not heal or any pigmented lump that begins to grow or bleed should be checked by a veterinarian immediately. Look out for mammary masses, changes in testicle size, discharge from the vulva or penis, increased or decreased urination, foul smelling or strangely colored urine, incontinence, swollen abdomen, black or bloody stool, change in appetite or water consumption, difficulty breathing, lethargy, gagging, or loss of balance.

To take your dog's temperature, lubricate a rectal thermometer (preferably the digital type), insert it about two inches (5 cm) into the dog's anus, and leave it for about one minute. Do not allow your dog to sit down on the thermometer! Normal temperature for a Whippet is around 101 degrees Fahrenheit (38.3°C), ranging from 100 to 102.5 degrees Fahrenheit (37.8°C to 39.2°C). Call your veterinarian if the temperature is over 104°F (40°C).

A good place to check the pulse is on the femoral artery, located inside the rear leg where the thigh meets the abdomen. Normal pulse rates range from 80 to 140 beats per minute in an awake Whippet and are strong and fairly regular.

Battle of the Bugs

Your Whippet's skin is its largest single organ and the one most accessible to you. It is a major interface between your dog and the environment and, as such, is vulnerable to a plethora of problems, many caused by fleas and ticks.

A healthy Whippet has clear eyes, clean ears, clean teeth, and an alert demeanor.

The Whippet's close hair makes any imperfections especially noticeable, but you should still feel for irregularities or bumps.

Ticks can be found anywhere on the dog, but most burrow around the ears, neck, chest, and between the toes. To remove a tick, use a tissue or tweezers since some diseases can be transmitted to humans. Grasp the tick as close to the skin as possible, and pull slowly and steadily, trying not to leave the head in the dog. Clean the site with alcohol. Often a bump will remain after the tick is removed, even if you got the head. It will go away with time. *Don't ever try to burn a tick out!* You may catch your dog on fire.

Fleas and ticks subject your dog to a myriad of health problems and considerable discomfort. Fleas can carry tapeworms, and ticks can carry Rocky Mountain spotted fever, tick paralysis, Lyme disease, babesiosis, and most commonly, tick fever (erlichiosis)—all serious diseases.

Recent advances in flea and tick control have finally put dog owners on the winning side. In any but the mildest of infestations, these new products are well worth their initial higher purchase price. Consider carefully the correct choice of products for your dog and situation:

• lufenuron (brand name: Program) is given as a pill once a month. Fleas that bite the dog and ingest the lufenuron in the dog's system are rendered sterile. It is extremely safe for the dog. All animals in the environment must be treated in order for the regime to be effective, however.

• imidacloprid (brand name: Advantage) is a liquid applied once a month on the animal's back. It gradually distributes itself over the entire skin surface and kills at least 98 percent of the fleas on the animal within 24 hours and will continue to kill fleas for a month. It can withstand water but not repeated swimming or bathing.

• fipronil (brand name: Frontline) comes either as a spray that you must apply all over the dog's body or as a

elf-distributing liquid applied only on
ne dog's back. Once applied, fipronil
ollects in the hair follicles and then
'icks out over time. Thus, it is resis-
ant to being washed off and can kill
eas for up to three months on dogs.
is also effective on ticks for a shorter
eriod.

pyriproxyfen (brand names: Nylar,
umilar, and others) is an insect
rowth regulator available as an ani-
nal or premise spray. It is marketed in
ifferent strengths and formulations. It
an protect in the home or yard for six
) 12 months and the animal for 100
ays, depending upon the particular
roduct.

Traditional flea control products are
ither less effective or less safe than
nese newer products. The perme-
rrins and pyrethrins are safe but have
irtually no residual action. The large
amily of cholinesterase inhibitors
)ursban, Diazinon, Malathion, Sevin,
;arbaryl, Pro-Spot, Spotton) last a lit-
e longer but have been known to kill
ogs when overused, when used in
ombination with cholinesterase-
hibiting yard products, or when used
vith cholinesterase-inhibiting deworm-
rs. You can identify a product con-
aining cholinesterase inhibitors by
ooking at the label. Such products are
ot recommended for use around
Vhippets. Incidentally, the ultrasonic
ea-repelling collars have been shown
) be both ineffective on fleas and irri-
rting to dogs. Scientific studies have
lso shown that feeding dogs brewer's
east or garlic, as has been advo-
ated for years by many dog owners,
; ineffective against fleas. However,
nany owners swear it works, and it
ertainly does no harm.

Do not use a flea collar on your
Vhippet! They can cause local irrita-
on and even systemic toxicity and
hould never be used on either Whip-
•ets or Greyhounds. Plus, they are
neffective.

A rubber grooming mitt removes dead hair, stimulates the skin, and feels heavenly.

A mitey problem: Two different
species of mites cause different forms
of mange in dogs. Sarcoptic mange
causes intense itching, often characterized by scaling of the ear tips. It is
highly contagious but easily cured with
an insecticidal dip.

Demodectic mange is not contagious but is far more difficult to cure.
The condition tends to run in families
and is more common in certain breeds
(but fortunately not in Whippets). It is
characterized by a moth-eaten
appearance, most often around the
eyes and lips. Demodectic mange
affecting the feet is also common and
can be extremely resistant to treatment. Most cases of demodectic
mange appear in puppies, usually
consisting of only a few patches that
often go away by themselves. However, in those cases that continue to
spread or in adult onset demodectic
mange, aggressive treatment using an
amitraz insecticidal dip is needed.
Your veterinarian will need to perform
a skin scraping to confirm the diagno-
sis before prescribing treatment. In
unresponsive cases, your veterinarian

may even prescribe daily administration of certain monthly heartworm preventatives, although this use is still considered *extralabel,* meaning that the drug has not been officially approved for that purpose or in that dosage.

Beauty Is Skin Deep

Flea allergy dermatitis (FAD) is the most common of all skin problems. Itchy, crusted bumps with hair loss in the region around the rump, especially at the base of the tail, result from a flea bite (actually, the flea's saliva) anywhere on the dog's body.

Besides FAD, dogs can have allergic reactions to pollens or other inhaled allergens. Allergies to weeds can manifest themselves between the dog's toes. Suspect them when you see the dog constantly licking its feet or when the feet are stained pink from saliva. Food allergies can also occur. New blood tests for antibodies are much easier and less expensive (though not as comprehensive) than the traditional intradermal skin testing.

Pyoderma, with pus-filled bumps and crusting, is another common skin disease. *Impetigo* is characterized by such bumps and crusting most often in the groin area of puppies. Both are treated with antibiotics and antibacterial shampoos.

A reddened, moist, itchy spot that suddenly appears is most likely a *hot spot,* which arises from an itch-scratch chew cycle resulting most commonly from fleas or flea allergy. Wash the area with an oatmeal-based shampoo, and prevent the dog from further chewing. Use an Elizabethan collar (available from your veterinarian or you can fashion one from a plastic pail), or an antichew preparation such as Bitter Apple (available from most pet stores). Your veterinarian can also prescribe anti-inflammatory medication. As a temporary measure, you can give your dog Benadryl—ask your veterinarian about dosage—which alleviates some itching and causes drowsiness. Both Benadryl and anti-inflammatory medication should decrease chewing.

In *seborrhea,* the dog may have excessive dandruff or greasiness, often with excessive earwax and rancid odor. Treatment is with antiseborrheic shampoos or diet change.

Hair loss may occur in a bilaterally symmetric pattern and without itching. This would be due to hypothyroidism, Cushing's syndrome, or testicular tumors.

Doggy odor is not only offensive; it is unnatural. Don't exile the dog or hold your breath. If a bath doesn't produce results, it's time to use your nose to sniff out the source of the problem. Infection is a common cause of bad odor; check the mouth, ears, feet, and genitals. Generalized bad odor can indicate a skin problem, such as seborrhea. Don't ignore bad odor, and don't make your dog take the blame for something you need to fix.

Give It Your Best Shot

Rabies, distemper, leptospirosis, canine hepatitis, parvovirus, and corona virus are highly contagious and deadly diseases that have broken many a loving owner's heart in the past. Now that vaccinations are available for these maladies, one would think they would no longer be a threat

Whippet Sense: Ouch!

Many Whippets can be amazingly stoic, even when they must be in pain. Because a dog may not be able to express that it is in pain, you must be alert to changes in your Whippet's demeanor. A stiff gait, low head carriage, reluctance to get up, irritability, dilated pupils, whining, or limping are all indications that your pet is in pain.

However, many dogs remain unvaccinated and continue to succumb to and spread these potentially fatal illnesses. Don't let your little Whippet be one of them.

Puppies receive their dam's immunity through nursing in the first days of life. This is why it is important that your pup's mother be properly immunized long before breeding and that your pup be able to nurse from its dam. The immunity gained from the mother will wear off after several weeks, and then the pup will be susceptible to disease unless you provide immunity through vaccinations. The problem is that there is no way to know exactly when this passive immunity will wear off, and vaccinations given before that time are ineffective. So you must revaccinate over a period of weeks so that your pup will not be unprotected and will receive effective immunity.

Your pup's breeder will have given the first vaccinations to your pup before it was old enough to go home with you. Bring all information about your pup's vaccination history to your veterinarian on your first visit so that the pup's vaccination schedule can be maintained. Meanwhile, it is best not to let your pup mingle with strange dogs.

Recent studies have implicated repeated vaccinations using vaccine combinations with some immune system problems. Some veterinarians thus recommend staggering different types of vaccines and discourage overvaccination. They also discourage vaccination in any dog that is under stress or not feeling well. Many dogs seem to feel under the weather for a day or so after getting their vaccinations, so don't schedule your appointment the day before boarding, a trip, or a big doggy event.

Vaccinations are also available for kennel cough and Lyme disease but may be optional depending upon your dog's lifestyle. In fact, in most parts of the country, the possibility of complications due to the Lyme vaccine are greater than the probability of problems due to actually contracting Lyme disease. Your veterinarian can advise you.

Internal Parasites

Internal parasites can rob your dog of vital nutrients, good health, and sometimes, even a long life. The most common internal parasites set up housekeeping in the intestines and heart.

Intestinal parasites: Hookworms, whipworms, ascarids, threadworms, and lungworms are all types of nematode parasites that can infect dogs of all ages but have their most devastating effects on puppies. When you take your dog to be vaccinated, bring along a stool specimen so that your veterinarian can also check for these parasites. Most puppies do have worms at some point, even pups from the most fastidious breeders. This is because some types of larval worms become encysted in the dam's body long before she ever became pregnant; perhaps when she herself was a pup. Here they lie dormant and immune

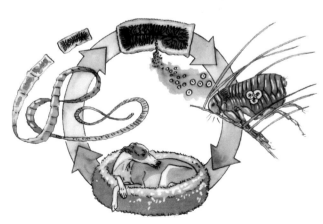

The life cycle of the tapeworm. Note that a flea is a necessary intermediate host.

from worming until hormonal changes due to her pregnancy cause them to be activated. Then they infect the dam's fetuses or her newborns through her milk. You may be tempted to pick up some worm medication and worm your puppy yourself but don't. Over-the-counter wormers are largely ineffective and often more dangerous than those available through your veterinarian. Left untreated, worms can cause vomiting, diarrhea, dull coat, listlessness, anemia, and death. Have your puppy regularly tested for internal parasites. Some heartworm preventives also prevent most types of intestinal worms (but not tapeworms).

Tapeworms (cestodes) tend to plague some dogs throughout their lives. No preventive exists except to rid your Whippet of fleas diligently because fleas transmit tapeworms to dogs. Tapeworms look like moving, white, flat worms on fresh stools or may dry up and look like rice grains around the dog's anus. Tapeworms are one of the least debilitating worms, but their segments can be irritating to the dog's anal region and are certainly unsightly.

Dog owners tend to have some strange ideas concerning worms. Let a dog scoot its rear on the ground, and its owner automatically diagnoses it as wormy. Although scooting may be a sign of tapeworms, a dog that repeatedly scoots more likely has impacted anal sacs. Somebody somewhere popularized the notion feeding a dog sugar and sweets will give it worms. Good reasons exist not to feed a dog sweets, but worms have nothing to do with them. Some companies have made a fortune at the expense of dog owners and their dogs by promoting the idea that dogs should be regularly wormed every month or so. Dogs should be wormed when, and only when, they have been diagnosed with worms. No worm medication is completely without risk, and it is foolish to use such medication carelessly.

Protozoa: Puppies and dogs also suffer from protozoan parasites, such as coccidia and especially, *Giardia*. These can cause chronic or intermittent diarrhea and can be diagnosed with a stool specimen. Because they are not worms, worm medications are ineffective. Your veterinarian can prescribe appropriate medication.

Heartworms: Heartworms are a deadly nematode parasite carried by mosquitoes. Wherever mosquitoes are present, dogs should be on heartworm prevention. Several effective types of heartworm preventive are available, some also prevent many other types of worms. Some require daily administration, while others require only monthly administration. The latter type is more popular and actually has a wider margin of safety and protection. They don't stay in the dog's system for a month but, instead, act on a particular stage in the heartworm's development. Giving the drug each month prevents any heartworms from ever maturing. In warm areas, your dog may need to be

Life cycle of heartworms. When a mosquito bites an infected dog, the mosquito ingests circulating immature heartworms, which it then passes on to the next dog it bites.

Good health care begins in puppyhood and lasts a lifetime.

in prevention year-round, but in milder climates, your dog may need to use prevention only during the warmer months. Your veterinarian can advise you about when your puppy should start and if year-round prevention is necessary in your area.

If you forget to give the preventive as prescribed, your dog may get heartworms. A dog with suspected heartworms should not be given the daily preventive because a fatal reaction could occur. The most common way of checking for heartworms is to check the blood for circulating microfilariae (the immature form of heart-worms), but this method may fail to detect the presence of adult heart-worms in as many as 20 percent of all tested dogs. An *occult* heartworm test, though slightly more expensive, tests for the presence of antigens to heart-worms in the blood and is more accurate. With either test, the presence of heartworms will not be detectable until nearly seven months after infection. Heartworms are treatable in their early stages, but the treatment is expensive and not without risks (although a less risky treatment has recently become available). If untreated, heartworms can kill your pet.

HOW-TO:
Health and Beauty

Cut the nails as close to the quick as possible.

Grooming is not only important for the sake of beauty. It also can prevent serious health problems.

Bathing: Dog skin has a pH of 7.5, while human skin has a pH of 5.5. Bathing a dog in a shampoo formulated for the pH of human skin can lead to scaling and irritation. Thus, you will generally get better results with a shampoo made for dogs. Most shampoos will kill fleas even if not especially formulated as a flea shampoo, but none has any residual killing action on fleas. So in general, flea shampoos are not a good buy.

Several therapeutic shampoos are available for various skin problems:
• dry, scaly skin: moisturizing shampoos
• excessive scale and dandruff: antiseborrheic shampoos
• damaged skin: antimicrobial shampoos
• itchy skin: oatmeal-based antipruritic shampoos

Remember that Whippets hate to be cold—or wet! Be sure to use warm water. Don't get water in the ears (try plug-

The dog's ear canal consists of an initial vertical canal, with an abrupt curve leading to a horizontal canal.

ging with cotton). Rinse thoroughly, towel dry, and then either bundle your Whippet up in a blanket, blow dry it, or keep it in a warm room.

Ears: The dog's ear canal is made of an initial long, vertical segment that then abruptly angles to run horizontally toward the skull. This configuration provides a moist environment in which various ear infections can flourish. The Whippet ear is well ventilated but can still sometimes fall prey to infections.

Signs of ear problems include inflammation, discharge, debris, foul odor, pain, scratching, shaking, tilting of the head, or circling to one side. Extreme pain may indicate a ruptured eardrum. Ear problems can be difficult to cure once they have become established, so early veterinary attention is crucial. Bacterial and fungal infections, ear mites or ticks, foreign bodies, inhalant allergies, seborrhea, or hypothyroidism are possible underlying problems. Grass awns are one of the most common causes of ear problems in dogs that spend time outdoors. Keep the ear lubricated with mineral oil, and seek veterinary treatment as

soon as possible. Ear problems can only get worse without proper treatment.

Don't stick cotton swabs down into the ear canal, as they can irritate the skin and pack debris into the horizontal canal. Never use powders in the ear, which can cake, or hydrogen peroxide, which leaves the ear moist.

Ear mites, which are often found in puppies, are highly contagious and intensely irritating. Affected dogs will shake their head, scratch their ears, and carry their head sideways. The ear mite's signature is a dark, dry, waxy buildup resembling coffee grounds in the ear canal, usually occurring in both ears. This material is actually dried blood mixed with earwax. If you place some of this wax on a piece of dark paper and have very good eyes or use a magnifying glass, you may be able to see the tiny, moving culprits. Over-the-counter ear mite preparations can cause worse irritation, so that ear mites are best treated by your veterinarian.

If you must treat the dog yourself, get a pyrethrin/mineral oil ear product. First flush the ear with an ear-cleaning solution. You can buy a solution

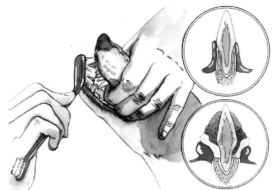

Brushing your dog's teeth will prevent costly dental procedures and disease. Left unattended, teeth can become seriously infected.

rom your veterinarian or make a mixture of one part alcohol to two parts white vinegar. Cleaning solutions will flush debris out will not kill mites or cure infections. Then apply the ear mite drops daily for at least a week and possibly a month. Because these mites are also found in the dog's fur all over its body, you should also bathe the pet weekly with a pyrethrin-based shampoo or apply a pyrethrin flea dip, powder, or spray. Separate a dog with ear mites from other pets, and wash your hands after handling its ears. Ideally, every pet in a household should be treated.

Many people automatically assume any ear problem is due to ear mites, but unless you actually see mites, don't treat the dog for them. You could make another problem worse.

Nails: An old saying states that a horse is no better than its feet. The same is true of a Whippet. Also, a Whippet's feet are no better than its nails. When you can hear the pitter-patter of clicking nails, the nails are hitting the floor with every step. When this happens, the bones of the foot are spread, causing discomfort and eventually splayed feet and lameness. If dewclaws are left untrimmed, they can get caught on things more easily or actually loop around and grow into the dog's leg. You must prevent this by trimming your dog's nails every week or two.

Begin by handling the feet and nails daily. Then cut the very tips of your puppy's nails every week, taking special care not to cut the quick (the central core of blood vessels and nerve

endings). You may find it easiest to cut the nails by holding the foot backward, much as a horse's hoof is held when being shoed. This way, your Whippet can't see what's going on, and you can see the bottom of the nail. Here you will see a solid core culminating in a hollowed nail. Cut the tip up to the core but not beyond. On occasion, you will slip up and cause the nail to bleed. This is best stopped by styptic powder, but if this is not available, dip the nail in flour or hold it to a wet tea bag.

Teeth: Tooth plaque and tartar are not only unsightly but contribute to bad breath and health problems. Dry food and hard dog biscuits, rawhide, and nylabone chewies are helpful, but not totally effective, at removing plaque. Brushing your Whippet's teeth once or twice weekly (optimally daily) with a child's toothbrush and doggy toothpaste is the best plaque remover. If not removed, plaque will attract bacteria and minerals, which will harden into tartar. If you cannot brush your Whippet's teeth, you may have to

have your veterinarian clean your dog's teeth as often as once a year.

Neglected plaque and tartar can cause infections to form along the gum line. The infection can gradually work its way down the sides of the tooth until the entire root is undermined. The tissues and bone around the tooth erode, and the tooth finally falls out. Meanwhile, the bacteria may have entered the bloodstream and traveled throughout the body, causing infection in the kidneys and heart valves. Neglecting your dog's teeth can do more harm than causing bad breath; it could possibly kill your dog.

Between four and seven months of age, Whippet puppies will begin to shed their baby teeth and show off new, permanent teeth. Often, deciduous (baby) teeth, especially the canines (fangs), are not shed, so that the permanent tooth grows in beside the baby tooth. If this condition persists for over a week, consult your veterinarian. Retained baby teeth can cause misalignment of adult teeth.

Neutering and Spaying

Another veterinary procedure that can save your pet's life is early spaying or neutering. If you don't intend to breed your pet—and more good reasons exist not to breed than to breed (see box)—plan to schedule this simple surgery before your pet reaches puberty, at least by eight or nine months of age. Not only will you not be contributing to the pet overpopulation problem, but you will be helping to safeguard your Whippet's life.

• Spaying (surgical removal of ovaries and uterus) before the first season drastically reduces the chances of breast or uterine cancer.

• Castration (surgical removal of the testicles) virtually eliminates the chance of testicular or prostate cancer.

1. Jejunum
2. Kidneys
3. Ureter
4. Descending colon
5. Ovaries
6. Uterine horn
7. Bladder
8. Vagina

Female reproductive organs. The ovary and uterus are removed in spaying.

1. Jejunum
2. Kidneys
3. Descending colon
4. Ureter
5. Bladder
6. Prostate gland
7. Testicle
8. Glans penis
9. Penis sheath
10. Bulbus glandis

Male reproductive organs. The testicles are removed in castration.

• Dogs with undescended testicles have an increased risk of testicular cancer and should be castrated before three to five years of age.

• In a recent study, 80 percent of all dogs killed by automobiles were intact (unneutered) males, apparently making their rounds.

Why breeding your Whippet is a bad idea:

• Many more good Whippets are born than there are good homes available. The puppy you sell to a less-than-perfect home may end up neglected, abused, discarded, or returned.

• Whippets typically have from five to seven puppies. Breeding so you can keep one pup ignores the fact that six others may not get a good home—or may be ransacking your home for the next ten years.

• Unless you Whippet has proven itself by earning titles and awards in competitions, you will have a difficult time finding buyers.

• Selling puppies will not come close to reimbursing you for the stud fee, prenatal care, whelping complications, Caesarian sections, supplemental feeding, puppy food, vaccinations, advertising, and staggering investment of time and energy.

• The bitch definitely experiences discomfort and some danger when whelping a litter. Watching a litter being born is not a good way to teach children the miracle of life; too many things can go wrong.

• Responsible breeders have spent years researching genetics and the breed, breed only the best specimens, and screen for hereditary defects in order to obtain superior puppies. Unless you have done the same, you are doing yourself, your dog, the puppies, any buyers, and the breed a great disservice.

A Pound of Cure

Your home care maintenance can go only so far in ensuring your pet's healthy status. No matter how diligent you are, eventually your Whippet will need professional medical attention. A good veterinarian will also be needed to monitor your dog's internal signs by way of blood tests and other procedures.

When choosing your veterinarian, consider availability, emergency arrangements, costs, facilities, and ability to communicate. Some veterinarians will include more sophisticated tests as part of their regular checkups. Such tests, while desirable, will add to the cost of a visit. Unless money is no object, reach an understanding about procedures and fees before having them performed. You and your veterinarian will form a team who will work together to protect your Whippet's health, so your rapport with your veterinarian is very important. Your veterinarian should listen to your observations and should explain to you exactly what is happening with your dog. The clinic should be clean and have safe, sanitary overnight accommodations. After-hours emergency arrangements should be made clear. A veterinarian who is familiar with the special needs of sighthounds is a real asset, so ask other sighthound owners about their vet.

Whippets and Anesthesia

The Whippet shares with its sighthound cousins a susceptibility to anesthesia problems. In the past, anesthetizing any sighthound involved considerable risks. At best, recovery from anesthesia was slower than that of other breeds; at worst, some dogs never recovered. Fortunately, the situation has vastly improved. With the use of up-to-date drugs and techniques, Whippet anesthesia is no longer a risky business.

Anesthetizing dogs typically involves two steps. An induction agent that renders the dog unconscious is administered first. Then an inhalant gas to maintain an anesthetized state is administered.

Many veterinarians still use induction agents that are not safe for Whippets. Barbiturate-containing or sulfur-containing anesthetics such as Pentothal should never be used with sighthounds. Sighthounds do not metabolize them as quickly as most dogs, probably because of differences in both liver metabolism and low body fat composition. Giving a lower dosage of these drugs, as some veterinarians do, is not a safe solution. Always insist that your veterinarian use a dissociative induction agent such as a ketamine/Valium mixture or similar agent, or even better, the human drug propofol.

Most veterinarians now use isoflurane as an inhalant agent to maintain anesthesia, and this is a safe agent for Whippets. You should specifically verify that your veterinarian will use it, however. It is more expensive than traditional inhalants and injectables, and some veterinarians may not routinely use it.

Whippets are also very sensitive to acepromazine, a drug often prescribed to calm down dogs. If used at all, it should be used at far lower dosages (at least one-half) than normally prescribed.

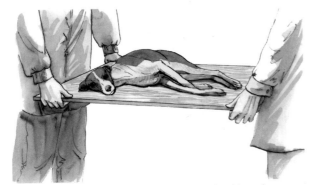
Move an injured dog carefully, preferably on a hard board. Use a blanket or towel if a board is not available.

If your veterinarian refuses to acknowledge that sighthounds have special anesthesia needs, seek the opinion of another vet. If your vet uses other agents, ask that the properties and advantages of these agents be explained to you before consenting to anesthesia for your Whippet.

In Case of Emergency

Even experienced dog owners have a difficult time deciding what constitutes a true emergency. When in doubt, err on the side of caution, and call the emergency clinic or your veterinarian for their opinion.

Be prepared: Because there are no paramedics for dogs, you must assume the role of paramedic and ambulance driver in case of an emergency. Now is the time to prepare for these life-saving roles. Know the phone number and location of the emergency veterinarian in your area. Keep the number next to the phone; don't rely on your memory during an emergency situation. Study the emergency procedures described in this chapter, and keep this guide handy. Misplaced instructions can result in the loss of critical time. Always keep enough fuel in your car to make it to the emergency clinic without stopping

for gas. Finally, stay calm. It will help you help your dog and will help your dog stay calm as well. A calm dog is less likely to go into shock. In general:

• Make sure you and the dog are in a safe location.

• Make sure breathing passages are open. Remove any collar and check the mouth and throat.

• Move the dog as little and as gently as possible.

• Control any bleeding.

• Check breathing, pulse, and consciousness.

• Check for signs of shock (very pale gums, weakness, unresponsiveness, faint pulse, shivering). Treat by keeping the dog warm and calm.

• Never use force or do anything that causes extreme discomfort.

• Never remove an impaled object (unless it blocks the airway).

For the following situations, administer first aid, and seek veterinary attention.

Poisoning: Symptoms and treatment vary depending upon the specific poison. In most cases, home treatment is not advisable. If in doubt about whether poison was ingested, call the veterinarian anyway. If possible, bring the poison and its container with you to the veterinarian.

Two of the most common and life-threatening poisons eaten by dogs are warfarin (rodent poison) and especially, ethylene glycol (antifreeze). Veterinary treatment must be obtained within two to four hours of ingestion of even tiny amounts if the dog's life is to be saved. *Do not wait for symptoms.*

Signs of poisoning vary according to the type of poison but commonly include vomiting, convulsions, staggering, and collapse. Call the veterinarian or poison control hotline, and give as much information as possible. Induce vomiting (except in the cases outlined below) by giving either hydrogen peroxide (mixed 1:1 with water), salt water, or dry mustard and water. Treat for shock, and get to the veterinarian at once. Be prepared for convulsions or respiratory distress.

Do not induce vomiting if the poison was an acid, alkali, petroleum product, solvent, cleaner, tranquilizer, or if a sharp object was swallowed; also do not induce vomiting if the dog is severely depressed, convulsing, comatose, or if over two hours have passed since ingestion. If the dog is not convulsing or unconscious, dilute the poison by giving milk, vegetable oil, or egg whites. Activated charcoal can adsorb many toxins. Baking soda or milk of magnesia can be given for ingested acids, and vinegar or lemon juice for ingested alkalis.

Seizures: A dog undergoing a seizure may drool, become stiff, or have uncontrollable muscle spasms. Wrap the dog securely in a blanket to prevent it from injuring itself on furniture or stairs. Remove other dogs from the area (they may attack the convulsing dog). Never put your hands (or anything) in a convulsing dog's mouth. Treat for shock. Make note of all characteristics and sequences of seizure activity, which can help to diagnose the cause.

Snakebites: Poisonous snakebites are characterized by swelling, discoloration, pain, fang marks, restlessness, nausea, and weakness. Restrain the dog and keep it quiet. Be able to describe the snake. Only if you can't get to the veterinarian immediately, apply a pressure bandage (not a tourniquet but a firm bandage) between the bite and the heart. If on a leg, keep it lower than the rest of the body. Most bites are on the head and are difficult to treat with first aid.

Allergic reaction: Insect stings are the most common cause of extreme reactions. Swelling around the nose and throat can block the airway. Other possible reactions include restless-

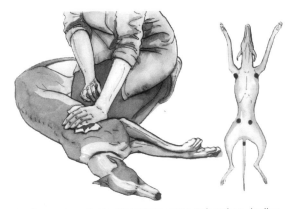

Apply pressure to the closest pressure point when dealing with uncontrolled bleeding of an extremity.

ness, vomiting, diarrhea, seizures, and collapse. If any of these symptoms occur, immediate veterinary attention will probably be necessary.

Bleeding: Consider wounds to be an emergency if they bleed profusely, are extremely deep, or if they open to the chest cavity, abdominal cavity, or head. Control massive bleeding first. Cover the wound with clean dressings and apply pressure; apply more dressings over the other dressings until the bleeding stops. Elevate the wound site, and apply a cold pack to the site. If at an extremity, apply pressure to the closest pressure point as follows:

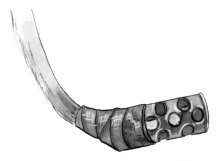

Tail tip: tape a hollow, well-ventilated hair curler over the tip of a damaged tail.

Who says sighthounds don't like water? Despite their short hair and love of heat, Whippets can easily overheat when running in warm weather. A cool dip can be lifesaving. Here a Whippet and a Greyhound make a splash.

- for a front leg: inside of front leg just above the elbow
- for a rear leg: inside of thigh where the femoral artery crosses the thigh bone
- for the tail: underside of tail close to where it joins the body

Cool a dog with heatstroke by covering it with wet towels and placing it in front of a fan or into cool water. Dunking the dog in ice water is dangerous because this constricts peripheral blood vessels.

Use a tourniquet only in life-threatening situations and when all other attempts have failed. Check for signs of shock.

Sucking chest wounds: Place sheet of plastic or other nonporous material over the hole. Bandage it to make as airtight a seal as possible.

Abdominal wounds: Place warm, wet, sterile dressing over any protruding internal organs; cover with bandage or towel. Do not attempt to push organs back into the dog.

Head wounds: Apply gentle pressure to control bleeding. Monitor for loss of consciousness or shock, and treat accordingly.

Burns: Deep burns, characterized by charred or pearly white skin with deeper layers of tissue exposed, are serious. Cool the burned area with cool packs, towels soaked in water, or by immersing in cold water. If over 50 percent of the dog is burned, do not immerse as this increases the likelihood of shock. Cover with a clean bandage or towel to avoid contamination. Do not apply pressure; do not apply ointments. Monitor for shock.

Electrical shock: A dog that chews an electric cord may collapse and have burns inside its mouth. Before touching the dog, disconnect the plug or cut power. If that cannot be done immediately, use a wooden pencil, spoon, or broom handle to knock the cord away from the dog. Keep the dog warm, and treat for shock. Monitor breathing and heartbeat.

Heatstroke: Rapid, loud breathing; abundant, thick saliva; bright red mucous membranes; and high rectal temperature are earlier signs of heatstroke. Later signs include unsteadiness, diarrhea, and coma. Wet the dog down and place it in front of a fan. If this is not possible, immerse the dog in cool water. *Do not plunge the dog in ice water;* the resulting constriction of peripheral blood vessels can make

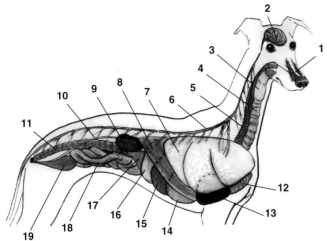

1. Sinus cavity
2. Brain
3. Thyroid cartilage
4. Trachea
5. Esophagus
6. Spinal cord
7. Lungs
8. Diaphragm
9. Kidneys
10. Ureter
11. Descending colon
12. Thymus
13. Heart
14. Liver
15. Stomach
16. Spleen
17. Pancreas
18. Jejunum
19. Bladder

Internal organs of the Whippet.

the situation worse. Offer small amounts of water for drinking. You must lower your dog's body temperature quickly, but do not lower it below 100 degrees Fahrenheit (37.8°C). Stop cooling the dog when the temperature reaches 103 degrees Fahrenheit (39.4°C).

Hypothermia: Shivering, feeling cold, and sluggishness are signs of a dog that has become excessively chilled. Later signs include a very low—under 95 degrees Fahrenheit (35°C)—body temperature, slow pulse and breathing rates, and coma.

Warm the dog gradually. Wrap it in a blanket (preferably one that has been warmed in the dryer). Place plastic bottles filled with hot water outside the blankets (not touching the dog). You can also place a plastic tarp over the blanket, making sure the dog's head is not covered. Monitor the temperature. Stop warming when the temperature reaches 101°F (38.3°C).

Hypoglycemia (low blood sugar): A dog with low blood sugar may appear disoriented, weak, staggering, and perhaps blind. Its muscles may twitch. Later stages lead to convulsions, coma, and death. Give food, or honey or syrup mixed with warm water.

Situations not described in this list can usually be treated with the same first aid as for humans. In all cases, the best advice is to seek the opinion of a veterinarian.

Know your plants—Whippets love to garden and graze, and some plants are poisonous.

HOW-TO:
ABCs of First Aid

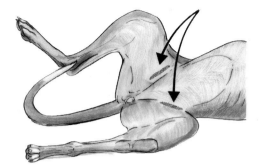

Check the pulse by feeling the femoral artery, located where the inner thigh meets the abdomen.

In an emergency, first check to see if the dog is responsive by calling its name or tapping on its head. If it is not, quickly access the ABCs of first aid: **A**irway, **B**reathing, and **C**irculation.

Airway: Make sure the airway is open. Extend the head and neck, open the mouth, and pull the tongue forward.

Breathing: Make sure the dog is breathing. Is the chest rising and falling? Can you feel exhaled air against your cheek? If not, give two rapid breaths through the nose before checking circulation.

Circulation: Check gum color, capillary refill time, and pulse. Gum color should be pink. When you press your thumb on the gum, it should regain its color within two seconds. Check the pulse by feeling either the heartbeat on the left side of the rib cage a couple of inches behind the elbow or feeling the pulse on the inside of the thigh, near the groin.

To check the airway, extend the dog's head and neck, open and clear the mouth, and pull the tongue forward.

If your dog has a pulse but is not breathing, administer artificial respiration.

If your dog does not have a pulse, administer cardiopulmonary resuscitation (CPR).

Artificial Respiration

1. Open dog's mouth, clear passage of secretions and foreign bodies.

2. Pull dog's tongue forward.

3. Seal your mouth over dog's nose and mouth, blow into dog's nose for two seconds, then release.

4. You should see your dog's chest expand; if not, try blowing with more force, making a tighter seal around the lips or checking for an obstruction.

5. Repeat at a rate of one breath every four seconds.

6. Stop every minute to monitor breathing and pulse.

7. If air collects in the stomach, push down just behind the rib cage every few minutes.

8. Continue until dog breathes on its own.

• For **obstructions,** wrap your hands around the abdomen, behind the rib cage, and compress briskly. Repeat if needed.

If the dog loses consciousness, extend the head and neck forward, pull the tongue out fully,

To empty a dog's lungs of water, suspend it upside down, and sway back and forth.

and explore the throat for any foreign objects.
• If due to **drowning,** turn dog upside down, holding around its waist, and sway back and forth so that water can run out of its mouth. Then administer mouth-to-nose respiration with the dog's head positioned lower than its lungs.

CPR

1. Place your hands, one on top of the other, on the left side of the chest about two inches (5 cm) up from and behind the point of the elbow.

2. Press down quickly and release.

3. Compress at a rate of about 100 times per minute.

4. After every 15 compressions, give two breaths through the nose. If you have a partner, the partner can give breaths every two or three compressions.

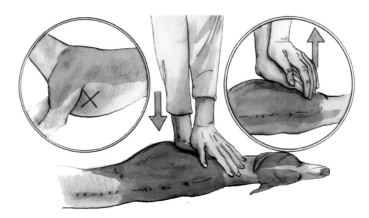

For CPR, place your hands, one on top of the other, on the left side of the chest about two inches (5 cm) up from and behind the point of the elbow. Then compress quickly and release.

Normal Values

Respiration	10–30 breaths/minute at rest
Pulse	60–120 beats/minute at rest
Temperature	101.5–102.5°F
Capillary refill time	Less than 2 seconds
Gum color	Pink (not white, red, bluish, yellowish, or with tiny red spots)
Hydration	Skin should pop back into position within 2 seconds of being lifted.

The Sick Whippet

Like people, dogs often feel under the weather. Sometimes it is not cause for alarm. However, if a problem persists for more than a couple of days, get your veterinarian's opinion. The following is an outline of the most common symptoms and some of their possible causes.

Vomiting: Vomiting is a common occurrence that may or may not indicate a serious problem. Vomiting after eating grass is common and usually of no great concern. Overeating is a common cause of occasional vomiting in puppies, especially if they play after eating. Feed smaller meals more frequently if this becomes a problem. Vomiting immediately after meals could indicate an obstruction of the esophagus. Repeated vomiting could indicate that the dog has eaten spoiled food or undigestible objects, or may have stomach illness. Veterinary advice should be sought. Meanwhile, withhold food (or feed as directed for diarrhea), and restrict water.

Consult your veterinarian immediately if your dog vomits a foul substance resembling fecal matter (indicating a blockage in the intestinal tract), blood (partially digested blood resembles coffee grounds), or if projectile or continued vomiting occur. Sporadic vomiting with poor appetite and generally poor condition could indicate internal parasites or a more serious internal disease that should also be checked by your veterinarian.

Diarrhea: Diarrhea can result from overexcitement or nervousness, a change in diet or water, sensitivity to certain foods, overeating, intestinal parasites, viral or bacterial infections, or ingestion of toxic substances. Bloody diarrhea, diarrhea with vomiting, fever, other signs of toxicity, or diarrhea that lasts for more than a day should not be allowed to continue without veterinary advice. Some of these could be symptomatic of potentially fatal disorders.

Less-severe diarrhea can be treated at home by withholding or severely restricting food and water for 24 hours. Ice cubes can be given to satisfy thirst. Administer human diarrhea medication in the same weight dosage as recommended for humans. A bland diet consisting of rice, tapioca, or cooked macaroni, along with cottage cheese or tofu for protein, should be given for several days. Feed nothing else. The intestinal tract needs time off in order to heal.

Coughing: Allergies, foreign bodies, pneumonia, parasites, tracheal collapse, tumors, and especially, kennel cough and heart disease, can all cause coughing.

Kennel cough is a highly communicable airborne disease caused by several different infectious agents. It is characterized by a gagging cough arising about a week after exposure. Inoculations are available and are an especially good idea if you plan to have your dog around other dogs at training classes or while being boarded.

Heart disease can result in coughing, most often following exercise or in the evening. Affected dogs will often lie down and point their nose in the air in order to breathe better.

Any persistent cough should be checked by your veterinarian. Coughing irritates the throat and can lead to secondary infections if allowed to continue unchecked. It can also be miserable for the dog.

Urinary tract diseases: If your dog has difficulty or pain in urination, urinates suddenly and often but in small amounts, or passes cloudy or bloody urine, it may be suffering from a problem of the bladder, urethra, or prostate. Dribbling of urine during sleep can indicate a hormonal problem. Urinalysis and a rectal exam by your veterinarian are necessary to diagnose the exact nature of the problem. Bladder infections must be treated promptly to prevent the infection from reaching the kidneys.

Blockage of urine can result in death. Inability to urinate requires immediate emergency veterinary attention.

Kidney disease, ultimately leading to kidney failure, is one of the most common ailments of older dogs. The earliest symptom is usually increased urination. Although the excessive urination may cause problems in keeping your house clean or your night's sleep intact, never try to restrict water from a dog with kidney disease. Increased urination can also be a sign of diabetes or a urinary tract infection. Your veterinarian can discover the cause with some simple tests, and each of these conditions can be treated. For kidney disease, a low-protein and low-sodium diet can slow the progression.

In males, infections of the *prostate gland* can lead to repeated urinary tract infections and sometimes painful defecation or blood and pus in the urine. Castration and long-term antibiotic therapy may be required for improvement.

Impacted anal sacs: Constant licking of the anus or scooting of the anus along the ground are characteristic signs of anal sac impaction. Dogs have two anal sacs that are normally emptied by rectal pressure during defecation. Their musky smelling contents may also be forcibly ejected when a dog is extremely frightened. Sometimes they fail to empty properly and become impacted or infected. This is more common in obese dogs, dogs with allergies or seborrhea, and dogs that seldom have firm stools. Impacted sacs cause extreme discomfort and can become infected. Treatment consists of manually emptying the sacs and administering antibiotics. As a last resort, the sacs may be removed surgically.

Endocrine disorders: The most widespread hormone-related disorders in the dog are diabetes, hypothyroidism, and Cushing's syndrome. The most common of these, *hypothyroidism,* also has the least obvious symptoms, which may include weight gain, lethargy, and coat problems such as oiliness, dullness, *symmetrical* hair loss, and hair that is easily pulled out.

The hallmark of *diabetes* is increased drinking and urination. Sometimes, increased appetite with weight loss occurs.

Cushing's syndrome (hyperadrenocorticism) is seen mostly in older dogs. It is characterized by increased drinking and urination, potbellied appearance, symmetrical hair loss on the body, darkened skin, and susceptibility to infections.

All of these conditions can be diagnosed with simple tests. They can be treated with drugs by your veterinarian.

Bites and stings: Dogs bite dogs. The problem with dog (or any animal) bites is that they are prone to infection. If your dog is bitten, allow some bleeding, then clean the area thoroughly and apply antibiotic ointment. A course of oral antibiotics will probably be necessary. It's best not to suture most animal bites, but a large one (over one-half inch in diameter) or one on the face or other prominent position may need to be sutured. Whippet skin is especially prone to lacerations and scarring, so expect your Whippet to need stitches sometime in its lifetime, whether due to a bite or snag.

Dogs are often stung by insects on their face or feet. Remove any visible stingers as quickly as possible. Administer baking soda and water paste to bee stings and vinegar to wasp stings. Clean the area, and apply antibacterial ointment. Keep an eye on the dog in case it has an allergic reaction, including swelling that could interfere with breathing or any change in consciousness. Call your veterinarian if you think the dog may be having a severe reaction.

Eye problems: Whippets have extremely healthy eyes, but even they can sometimes have problems. Squinting or tearing can be due to an irritated cornea or foreign body. Examine under the lids and flood the eye with saline solution, or use a moist cotton swab to remove any debris. If no improvement is seen after a day, have your veterinarian take a look. A watery discharge without squinting can be a symptom of allergies or a tear drainage problem. A clogged tear drainage duct can cause the tears to drain onto the face rather than the normal drainage through the nose. Your veterinarian can diagnose a drainage problem with a simple test.

For contact with eye irritants, flush the eye for five minutes with water or saline solution. For injuries, cover with clean gauze soaked in water or saline solution.

As your Whippet ages, the lens of the eye naturally becomes a little hazy. You will notice this as a slightly grayish appearance behind the pupils. However, if this occurs at a young age or if the lens looks white or opaque, ask your veterinarian to check your dog for *cataracts*. In cataracts, the lens becomes so opaque that light can no longer reach the retina; as in humans, the lens can be surgically replaced with an artificial lens.

Any time your dog's pupils do not react to light or when one eye reacts differently from another, take it to the veterinarian immediately. It could indicate a serious ocular or neurological problem.

The eyes are such complex and sensitive organs that you should always err on the side of caution. Consult your veterinarian at the slightest sign of a problem.

The Medicine Chest
- rectal thermometer
- scissors
- tweezers
- sterile gauze dressings
- self-adhesive bandage (such as Vet-Wrap)
- instant cold compress
- antidiarrheal medication
- ophthalmic ointment
- soap
- antiseptic skin ointment
- hydrogen peroxide
- clean sponge
- penlight
- syringe
- towel
- stethoscope (optional)
- oxygen (optional)
- first aid instructions
- veterinarian's, emergency clinic's, and poison control center's phone numbers

Medications
When giving pills, open your dog's mouth and place the pill well to the back and in the middle of the tongue. Close the mouth, and gently stroke the throat until your dog swallows. Pre-wetting capsules or covering them with cream cheese or some other food helps prevent capsules from sticking to the tongue or roof of the mouth. For liquid medicine, tilt the head back, keep the dog's mouth almost (but not quite tightly) closed, and place the liquid in the pouch of the cheek. Then hold the mouth closed until the dog swallows. Always give the full course of medications prescribed by your veterinarian. Don't give your dog human medications unless you have been directed to do so by your veterinarian. Some medications for humans have no effect upon dogs, and some can have a very detrimental effect.

The Friend of a Lifetime

You and your Whippet have a lifetime of experiences to share. Your life may change dramatically in the years to come: marriage, divorce, new baby, new home—for better or worse your Whippet will still depend on you and still love you. Always remember the promise you made to yourself and your future puppy before you made the commitment to share your life: to keep your interest in your dog and care for it every day of its life with as much love and enthusiasm as you did the first day it arrived home.

Remember, too, that your Whippet will change through the years. The Whippet's lithe body shape and natural athleticism sometimes mislead owners into forgetting that Whippets, like all dogs, get old. One day you will look at your young whippersnapper and be shocked to discover its face has silvered and its gait has stiffened. It sleeps longer and more soundly than it did as a youngster and is slower to get going. It may be less eager to play and more content to lie in the sun. Getting your dog to healthy old age is a worthy accomplishment. Just make sure that you appreciate all the stages along the way.

Every stage of a Whippet's life is its best. Puppies are so full of curiosity and mischief, adolescents begin to blossom into adults, and adults mature into truly dependable companions. Anyone who has had a Whippet for its entire life, however, would probably assert that the senior Whippet is the best. With the wisdom of years, the Whippet becomes almost humanlike in its ability to tune in to your emotions. The older Whippet, its ears often standing erect due to the hardening of the cartilage, its eyes often hazy due to cataracts, its gait stiff, and its face gray, is in the opinion of many Whippet fanciers, the most beautiful Whippet of all.

Aging Gracefully

It is important to keep your older Whippet relatively active. Both physical activity and metabolic rates decrease in older animals, meaning that they require fewer calories to maintain the same weight. Older dogs that continue to be fed the same as when they were young risk becoming obese; such dogs have a greater risk of cardiovascular and joint problems.

Introducing a new puppy or pet may be welcomed and encourage your dog to play. However, if your dog is not used to other dogs, the newcomer will more likely be resented and be an additional source of stress. Some older dogs become cranky and less patient, especially when dealing with puppies or boisterous children. Don't just excuse behavioral changes, especially if sudden, as due simply to aging. They could be symptoms of pain or disease.

Long trips may be grueling, and boarding in a kennel may be extremely upsetting. The immune system may be less effective in older dogs, so shielding your dog from infectious disease, chilling, overheating, and any stressful conditions is increasingly important.

Older dogs may experience hearing or vision loss. Be careful not to startle a dog with impaired senses, as a startled dog could snap in self-defense.

The promise of a lifetime.

The slight haziness that appears in the older dog's pupils is normal and has minimal effect upon vision, but some dogs, especially those with diabetes, may develop cataracts. These can be removed by a veterinary ophthalmologist if they are severe. Dogs with gradual vision loss can cope well as long as they are kept in familiar surroundings and extra safety precautions are followed.

In general, any ailment that an older dog has is magnified in severity compared with the same symptoms in a younger dog. Some of the more common symptoms and their possible causes in older Whippets include:
• diarrhea: kidney or liver disease, pancreatitis
• coughing: heart disease, tracheal collapse, lung cancer
• difficulty eating: periodontal disease, oral tumors
• decreased appetite: kidney disease, liver disease, or heart disease, pancreatitis, cancer
• increased appetite: diabetes, Cushing's syndrome
• weight loss: heart disease, liver disease, or kidney disease, diabetes, cancer
• abdominal distention: heart or kidney disease, Cushing's syndrome, tumor
• increased urination: diabetes, kidney or liver disease, cystitis, Cushing's syndrome
• limping: arthritis, patellar luxation
• nasal discharge: tumor, periodontal disease

Vomiting and diarrhea in an older dog can signal many different problems. Keep in mind that a small, older dog cannot tolerate the dehydration that results from continued vomiting or diarrhea, and you should not let it continue unchecked. The older dog should see its veterinarian at least twice a year. Blood tests can detect early stages of diseases that can benefit from treatment.

Older dogs present a somewhat greater anesthesia risk. Most of this increased risk can be negated, however, by first screening dogs with a complete medical workup.

Older dogs tend to have a stronger body odor, but don't just ignore increased odors. They could indicate specific problems, such as periodontal disease, impacted anal sacs, seborrhea, ear infections, or even kidney disease. Any strong odor should be checked by your veterinarian. Like people, dogs lose skin moisture as they age, and though dogs don't have to worry about wrinkles, their skin can become dry and itchy. Regular brushing can help by stimulating oil production.

Although some geriatric dogs are overweight, many Whippets lose weight and may need to eat puppy food in order to keep the pounds on. Most older dogs do not require a special diet unless they have a particular medical need for it (for example, obesity: low calorie; kidney failure: low protein; heart failure: low sodium).

Older dogs should be fed several small meals instead of one large meal and should be fed on time. Moistening dry food or feeding canned food can help a dog with dental problems enjoy its meal.

While Whippets of any age enjoy a soft, warm bed, it is an absolute necessity for older Whippets. Arthritis is a common cause of intermittent stiffness and lameness. It can be helped with heat, a soft bed, moderate exercise, and possibly drug therapy.

If you are lucky enough to have an older Whippet, you still must accept that an end will come. Heart disease, kidney failure, and cancer eventually claim most of these senior citizens. Early detection can help delay their effects but, unfortunately, can seldom prevent them.

As your Whippet ages, attention to its health and comfort become even more vital.

Saying Farewell

Despite the best of care, a time will come when neither you nor your veterinarian can prevent your cherished pet from succumbing to old age or an incurable illness. It seems hard to believe that you will have to say good-bye to someone who has been such a focal point of your life, in truth, a real member of your family. That dogs live such a short time compared with humans is a cruel fact, but one that you must ultimately face.

You should realize that both of you have been fortunate to have shared so many good times, but make sure that your Whippet's remaining time is still pleasurable. Many terminal illnesses make your dog feel very ill, and there comes a point where your desire to keep your friend with you as long as possible may not be the kindest thing for either of you. If your dog no longer eats its dinner or treats, this is a sign that it does not feel well, and you must face the prospect of doing what is best for your beloved friend.

Euthanasia is a difficult and personal decision that no one wishes to make and no one can make for you. Ask your veterinarian if there is a reasonable chance of your dog getting better and if it is likely that your dog is suffering. Ask yourself if your dog is getting pleasure out of life and if it enjoys most of its days. Financial considerations can be a factor if it means going into debt in exchange for just a little while longer. Your own emotional state must also be considered.

If you do decide that euthanasia is the kindest farewell gesture for your beloved friend, discuss with your veterinarian beforehand what will happen. Euthanasia is painless and involves giving an overdose of an anesthetic. If your dog is scared of the veterinary clinic, you might feel better having the doctor meet you at home or come out to your car. Although it won't be easy, try to remain with your dog so that its last moments will be filled with your love; otherwise have a friend that your Whippet knows stay with it. Try to recall the wonderful times you have shared, and realize that however painful losing such a once-in-a-lifetime

Whippet Snippet:
The Healing Touch

Whippets excel at many roles, but perhaps one of the most important is that of canine therapist. As more of the population becomes elderly and either unable to care for or keep a pet, the result is particularly sad for lonely people who may have relied upon the comfort and companionship of a pet throughout most of their independent years. Studies have shown that pet ownership increases life expectancy, and petting animals can lower blood pressure. In recent years, nursing home residents have come to look forward to visits by dogs, including many Whippets. These dogs must be meticulously well mannered and well groomed. To be registered as a Certified Therapy Dog, a dog must demonstrate that it will act in an obedient, outgoing, gentle manner to strangers. The Whippet combines the prefect blend of attributes for this most vital job: they are amiable without being overwhelming, startlingly beautiful, and just the right size for a little cuddle.

Whippet therapy consists of a wet tongue, a cool nose, and a warm heart.

dog is, it is better than never having had such a partner at all.

Many people who regarded their Whippet as a member of the family nonetheless feel embarrassed at the grief they feel at its loss. Yet this dog has often functioned as a surrogate child, best friend, and confidant. Partnership with a pet can be one of the closest and most stable relationships in many people's lives. Because people are often closer to their pets than they are to distant family members, it is not uncommon to feel more grief at the loss of the pet. Unfortunately, the support from friends that comes with human loss is too often absent with pet loss. Such well-meaning but ill-informed statements as "He was just a dog," or, "Just get another one," do little to ease the pain. However, the truth is that many people simply don't know how to react and probably aren't really as callous as they might sound. Many people, however, share your feelings, and pet bereavement counselors are available at many veterinary schools.

After losing such a cherished friend, many people say they will never get another dog. True, no dog will ever take the place of your dog. But you will find that another Whippet is a welcome diversion and will help keep you from dwelling on the loss of your first pet, as long as you don't keep comparing the new dog with the old. True also, by getting another dog, you are sentencing yourself to the same grief in another ten to 15 years, but wouldn't you rather have that than miss out on a second once-in-a-lifetime dog?

Choosing to add a Whippet to your home means devoting a significant part of your life to this little dog. The loss of a companion may mark the end of an era for you, a time when you and your Whippet grew up or grew old together. One could scarcely ask for a better life partner, though, than the Whippet, a fast friend with a heart racing with love.

Appendix: The Official AKC Standard For the Whippet

General appearance: A medium size sighthound giving the appearance of elegance and fitness, denoting great speed, power, and balance without coarseness. A true sporting hound that covers a maximum of distance with a minimum of lost motion. Should convey an impression of beautifully balanced muscular power and strength combined with great elegance and grace of outline. Symmetry of outline, muscular development, and powerful gait are the main considerations; the dog being built for speed and work, all forms of exaggeration should be avoided.

Size, proportion, substance: Ideal height for dogs, 19 to 22 inches (48 to 56 cm); for bitches, 18 to 21 inches (46 to 53 cm), measured at the highest point of the withers. More than one-half inch (1.2 cm) above or below the stated limits will disqualify. Length from forechest to buttocks equal to or slightly greater than height at the withers. Moderate bone throughout.

Head: Keen, intelligent expression. *Eyes* large and dark. Both eyes must be of the same color. Yellow or light eyes should be strictly penalized. Blue or wall eyes shall disqualify. Fully pigmented eyelids are desirable.

Rose ears, small, fine in texture; in repose, thrown back and folded along neck. Fold should be maintained when at attention. Erect ears should be severely penalized. *Skull* long and lean, fairly wide between the ears, scarcely perceptible stop.

Muzzle should be long and powerful, denoting great strength of bite, without coarseness. Lack of underjaw should be strictly penalized. Nose entirely black.

Teeth of upper jaw should fit closely over teeth of lower jaw, creating a scissors bite. Teeth should be white and strong. Undershot shall disqualify. Overshot one-quarter inch (0.6 cm) or more shall disqualify.

Neck, topline, body: Neck long, clean, and muscular, well arched with no suggestion of throatiness, widening gracefully into the top of the shoulder. A short, thick neck or a ewe neck should be penalized.

The *back* is broad, firm, and well muscled, having length over the loin. The back line runs smoothly over the withers with a graceful, natural arch not too accentuated, beginning over the loin and carrying through over the croup; the arch is continuous without flatness. A dip behind shoulder blades, wheel back, flat back, or a steep or flat croup should be penalized.

Brisket very deep, reaching as nearly as possible to the point of the elbow. *Ribs* well sprung but with no suggestion of barrel shape. The space between the forelegs is filled in so that there is no appearance of a hollow between them. There is a definite tuck up of the underline.

The *tail* long and tapering, reaching to the hip bone when drawn through between the hind legs. When the dog

1. Muzzle
2. Stop
3. Occuipt of skull
4. Crest of neck
5. Withers
6. Back
7. Loin
8. Croup
9. Thigh
10. Second thigh
11. Hock
12. Rear pastern
13. Foot
14. Stifle
15. Tail
16. Flank
17. Tuck
18. Ribcage
19. Elbow
20. Front pastern
21. Forearm
22. Upper arm
23. Shoulder

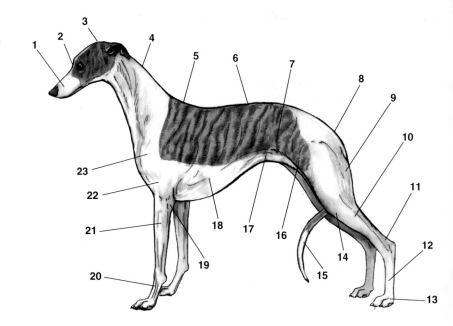

Whippet anatomy.

is in motion, the tail is carried low with only a gentle upward curve; tail should not be carried higher than top of back.

Forequarters: *Shoulder blade* long, well laid back, with flat muscles, allowing for moderate space between shoulder blades at peak of withers. Upper arm of equal length, placed so that the elbow falls directly under the withers.

The points of the elbows should point neither in nor out but straight back. A steep shoulder, short upper arm, heavily muscled or loaded shoulder, or a very narrow shoulder, all of which restrict low, free movement, should be strictly penalized.

Forelegs straight, giving appearance of strength and substance of bone. Pasterns strong, slightly bent, and flexible. Bowed legs, tied in elbows, legs lacking substance, legs set far under the body so as to create an exagger-

ated fore chest, or weak or upright pasterns should be strictly penalized.

Both front and rear feet must be well formed with hard, thick pads. Feet more hare than cat, but both are acceptable. Flat, splayed, or soft feet without thick, hard pads should be strictly penalized. Toes should be long, close, and well arched. Nails strong and naturally short or of moderate length. Dewclaws may be removed.

Hindquarters: Long and powerful. The thighs are broad and muscular, stifles well bent; muscles are long and flat, and carry well down toward the hock. The hocks are well let down and close to the ground. Sickle or cow hocks should be strictly penalized.

Coat: Short, close, smooth, and firm in texture. Any other coat shall be a disqualification. Old scars and injuries, the result of work or accident, should not be allowed to prejudice the dog's chance in the show ring.

Color: Color immaterial.

Gait: Low, free moving, and smooth, with reach in the forequarters and strong drive in the hindquarters. The dog has great freedom of action when viewed from the side; the forelegs must move forward close to the ground to give a long, low reach; the hind legs have strong propelling power. When moving and viewed from front or rear, legs should turn neither in nor out, nor should feet cross or interfere with each other.

Lack of front reach or rear drive, or a short, hackney gait with high wrist action, should be strictly penalized. Crossing in front or moving too close should be strictly penalized.

Temperament: Amiable, friendly, gentle, but capable of great intensity during sporting pursuits.

Disqualifications:
• More than one-half inch (1.2 cm) above or below stated height limits.
• Blue or wall eyes.
• Teeth undershot or overshot one-quarter inch (0.6 cm) or more.
• Any coat other than short, close, smooth, and firm in texture.

Standard Terms
• **coarseness:** heavy, thick bone; not graceful
• **withers:** highest point of the shoulders
• **forechest:** chest protruding in front of shoulder assembly
• **wall-eyes:** eyes with a whitish iris
• **rose ears:** a small ear that folds back on itself
• **undershot:** the front teeth (incisors) of the lower jaw are positioned in front of the front teeth of the upper jaw when the mouth is closed
• **overshot:** the front teeth (incisors) of the upper jaw protrude beyond the front teeth of the lower jaw when the mouth is closed
• **throatiness:** excessive loose skin under the throat

The Whippet resembles a Greyhound in miniature, with a curvaceous slender build.

• **ewe neck:** reverse curvature of the neck so that the top has a concave curve and the underside is bowed out
• **wheel back:** overly rounded back line, usually beginning too far forward toward the withers
• **tuckup:** markedly smaller waist
• **well laid back shoulders:** the angle of the shoulder blade is as close to 45 degrees as possible in relation to the vertical
• **steep shoulders:** shoulder blades positioned too vertically
• **loaded shoulders:** shoulder blades shoved out from the body because of overdevelopment of the underlying musculature
• **harefeet:** elongated feet
• **cat feet:** round feet
• **stifles:** knees
• **sickle hocks:** hocks that do not fully extend when moving
• **cow hocks:** hocks that point toward each other when viewed from the rear
• **hackney:** movement in which excessively high front action occurs.

Useful Addresses and Literature

Organizations

American Kennel Club
51 Madison Avenue
New York, NY 10010
(212) 696-8200

AKC Registration and
    Information
5580 Centerview Drive, Ste 200
Raleigh, NC 27606-3390
(919) 233-9767

American Whippet Club
10177 Blue River Hills Road
Manhattan, KS 66503

American Whippet Club
National Rescue Chairperson
Peggy Bush
1201 Keats Drive
Dallas, TX 75211
(214) 337-1758

American Sighthound Field
    Association
Sean McMichael,
    Corresponding Secretary
2848 Alpin Road
Crestview, FL 32539
(860) 563-0533
(newcomers' information)

Home Again Microchip Service
1-800-LONELY-ONE

Magazines

Dog Fancy
P.O. Box 53264
Boulder, CO 80322-3264
(303) 666-8504

Dogs USA Annual
P.O. Box 55811
Boulder, CO 80322-5811
(303) 786-7652

Dog World
29 North Wacker Drive
Chicago, IL 60606-3298
(312) 726-2802

AKC Gazette
51 Madison Avenue
New York, NY 10010

ASFA Field Advisory News
Vicky Clarke
P.O. Box 399
Alpaugh, CA 93201

Whippet World
4401 Zephyr Street
Wheat Ridge, CO 80033-3299

Sighthound Review
10177 Blue River Hills Road
Manhattan, KS 66503

Whippet World
3 Poole Street
Cavendish, Suffolk, C010 8BE
    England

Whippet Wrunner
13765 South 1300 West
Riverton, UT 84065

Books

Bengtson, Bo. *The Whippet*.
    MIP Publishing, Montecito,
    CA. 1994.
Douglas-Todd, C. H. *The Whip-
    pet*. Popular Dogs Publishing,
    England. 1973.
Gilmour, Patsy. *Whippets
    Today*. Howell Book House,
    New York. 1994.
Hutchinson, William. *Hutchin-
    son on Sighthounds*. (Reprint
    of the sighthound sections
    from *Hutchinson's Dog Ency-
    clopedia,* originally published
    1934). Hoflin Publishing,
    Wheat Ridge, CO. 1976.
Miller, Constance. *Gazehounds:
    The Search for Truth*. Hoflin
    Publishing, Wheat Ridge,
    CO. 1988. (History of all
    sighthounds).
Pegram, Lois. *The Complete
    Whippet*. Howell Book House.
    1976. (Out of print).
Rawlings, Shirley. *Whippets*.
    Crowood Press, England.
    1991.
Walsh, E. O. & Lowe, Mary.
    The English Whippet. Boydell
    Press, England. 1984.

Video

AKC Whippet Breed Video
    #VVT419
American Kennel Club
Attn: Video Fulfillment
5580 Centerview Drive
Suite 200
Raleigh, NC 27606
(919) 233-9780

ndex

W hippets love the
great outdoors,
especially in the spring.